Looking......

Good

LOOKING GOOD

The ultimate teenage beauty guide

Vickie Bramwell

Piccadilly Press • London

Phototypeset and designed from author's disk by Rebecca Elgar with Maria D'Orsi.

Illustrations by Zena Flax
Printed and bound by Progressive Printing Ltd., Leigh-on-Sea, for the publishers Piccadilly Press Ltd., 5 Castle Road, London NW1 8PR

A catalogue record for this book is available from the British Library

ISBN: 1 85340 352 0 (trade paperback)
1 85340 357 1 (hardback)

Vickie Bramwell is a freelance journalist specialising in beauty and health. She was the Lifestyle Editor of *Hello!* magazine and contributes regularly to national newspapers and women's magazines. She now lives in New York and London.

For my bright and beautiful niece,
Claire Beatson

Everybody likes looking good.

It's one of those facts of life.

We should all try to make ourselves look good. Everyone can be attractive even if they aren't blessed with perfect features – and not many of us are. Making the most of your looks shows that you care about yourself and that is always attractive to others. It makes you feel good and it can give you bags of confidence. Just think: if you know that the outside is up to scratch then you feel more confident and relaxed inside, and this shows up in how you act. It's one less thing to worry about if you like, and also something to be proud of.

> **"YOU make yourself look good by playing up your best points and disguising those you don't like."**

This book isn't going to tell you how to have the most perfect face or drop dead gorgeous figure. It's certainly not about spending hours in front of the mirror carefully applying layers of make-up. That's not what true beauty is about.

What it *will* tell you is how to be a naturally more attractive person, how to make the most of yourself and become more confident in your looks. And believe it or not it can be quite simple. It's often free, too. Don't believe me? Then let me tell you first my best and most stunning beauty trick:

a smile

That's right, just an ordinary common-or-garden smile! It's been scientifically proven (yes, people in white coats have studied the effects!) that those who smile make others think that they're brighter, prettier and friendlier than those who don't. And a simple smile can also make you feel happier, even when you're down in the dumps. A good chuckle releases some things called endorphins in the body. They're our own 'happy' chemicals and they lift our spirits. So why not give it a whole-hearted go?

It could work wonders.

What have you got to Lose?

That was a particularly quick looking good trick, but there are many more just as easy as well as a few where you need to concentrate a bit more. Let's get down to some more self-improvement tactics. Let's look good and let's have **fun** while we're doing it!

CHAPTER ONE

making HEADLINES

Hair is called your crowning glory. Now that may be a bit poetic for what's on top of your head, but it can be a real asset. You can make even the most pitiful-looking top-knot something to be proud of.

Sporting healthy, shiny-looking hair is one of the simplest ways to improve your general appearance. After all, it's one of the first things that other people notice about you. Just think, when you describe other people, what do you say? The girl with the blue eyes? The one with the large feet? No, hair is usually the first thing that comes to mind.

Your hair is dead except for the roots. It can't feel and say 'ooch' when it's getting damaged (luckily, or we'd have a hard time cutting it!). And it can't repair itself like other living parts of the body such as the skin. So, just like a woollen sweater, hair needs tender, loving care when washing and styling it to keep it in good condition.

So your particular crown may be a short trendy bob, long flowing locks, a face framing halo or just a complete mess. Here are some steps to make it, and keep it, one of your greatest assets.

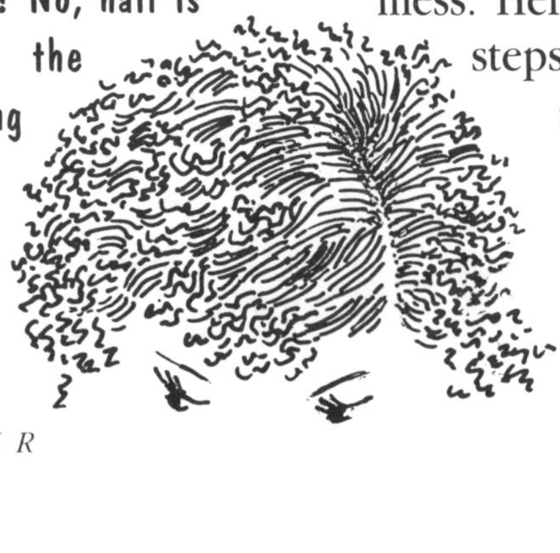

head turning

how to get the best looking hair at home

Wash

We all know how to wash our hair, don't we? Wrong! It may seem as if it takes a long time simply to get clean hair but it's worth it for the extra shine and compliments. Here's how people who care for their hair get the **best shine**. You can wash it as often as you like; every day if you feel like it needs it:

1. Wet your hair thoroughly with warm water.

2. Apply a fifty pence piece size of shampoo in bits all over your head, as near to your scalp as possible. If you've got long thick hair, make partings all over your head and apply the shampoo in small dribbles along them.

3

Gently massage the shampoo in with the soft pads of your fingertips at your scalp so as not to scratch with your nails.

4

Scrunch the lather through your hair.

5

Rinse it off in clear warm water (running from a shower or shower attachment is best) for two minutes, gently wringing it out all the time. Two minutes is a long time for rinsing, but it makes sure you get rid of all the soapy residue that can make hair look dull and dry your scalp. If you're not sure how long, time it.

6

ONE SHAMPOO SHOULD BE ENOUGH, BUT IF YOUR HAIR IS VERY DIRTY AND HASN'T BEEN WASHED FOR A FEW DAYS, REPEAT THE PROCESS.

7

Now pat it with a towel so it's not dripping wet and go to work on the shine.

Condition

We use conditioner to smooth down the minuscule, overlapping tiles on our hair, called cuticles. They can only be seen under a microscope. A smoother hair surface gives more light reflecting shine.

1

Rub a fifty pence piece size of conditioner between your palms and stroke it on to the hair near your scalp downwards to the tips. Avoid the roots which are supplied with natural conditioners from your scalp (which are what eventually makes it greasy, too).

2

Comb your hair through with a wide toothed comb to spread the conditioner evenly, making sure you don't pull any tangles.

3

Leave it on for as long as the bottle recommends (usually at least a minute).

4

Rinse again for two whole minutes.

5

Comb it through, starting with small strokes at the ends and working up to the roots. This prevents pulling any tangles which would damage hair.

Hair is more elastic and weaker and so more likely to break when it's wet.

HEADY STUFF

Forget about feeding your stomach from the fridge, how about trying to nourish your hair and scalp instead! If you want an extra special treatment for your hair once a week, everyday foods found in most larders can act as great conditioners.

Choose the edible conditioner to suit your hair. Apply all of these, except the first one, *before* washing your hair:

Greasy hair

Greasy hair looks flatter and sticky the day after washing. Choose either vinegar, citrus fruit (like lemon, lime or orange) or beer. Pour two tablespoons evenly over already dampened hair to help wash away oiliness almost immediately. They will also give your hair a great shine. Rinse thoroughly afterwards – unless you like the smell!

DRY HAIR

Dry hair looks dull and breaks off easily. Mash up an avocado. Now put it on a comb and comb it evenly through dry hair. Wrap your head (not your face!) in cling film. Do something else for fifteen minutes minimum – trying not to be seen unless you like a weird reputation!

DRY HAIR AND SCALP

Flaky hair means your scalp is flaking from dryness, dandruff or a skin complaint (see Trouble-shooting section). Carefully massage two teaspoons of cooking oil through your hair, distributing it as evenly as possible.
Wash it off thoroughly after two minutes.

FRIZZY HAIR

Frizzy hair is wild and unmanageable and can look dull without good conditioning. Try two tablespoons of mayonnaise on your comb. When it's evenly distributed, spend fifteen minutes sporting that attractive cling film turban again!

SORE OR STINGING SCALP FROM DRYNESS OR SUNBURN

Put dollops of natural plain yoghurt as near to your scalp as possible. Leave it on for as long as you (or others) can bear it before washing off.

greasy hair and no time to wash it

There are some good spray-in-brush-out dry shampoos at chemists, but they can make dark hair look a bit dusty. If you've got dark hair, try soaking a cotton wool ball with the diluted juice of a lemon or lime. Strain the juice then add a teaspoon to half a cup of warm water. Using a cotton wool ball, dab it over your scalp in greasy partings to bring back the shine.

For lighter coloured hair which you don't have time to wash, talcum powder is an alternative. It's kinder to your scalp to go for an unfragranced or baby one. Sprinkle a small amount evenly through your hair. Gently massage it in and then brush it out thoroughly to help return the shine.

A hasty word of advice: don't put someone's dinner on your head! Annoyed *and* hungry could make a powerful explosion in a person. Ask a parent before relocating kitchen items to the bathroom.

Flyaway or full of electricity after drying

Fine hair tends to be flyaway and won't hold a style for long. You can buy hair serums in the shops. A tiny drop of these, rubbed between your palms and smoothed over the surface, coats the top hair and helps bring it back to earth. Any cooking oil, but preferably one that doesn't smell and attract the flies (like olive oil would), will work just as well.

A TINY DROP REMEMBER!

H e a d ★ d r e ss e s

If you let your hair dry naturally you don't need any styling aids, such as mousses, gels or sprays to set it in any distinctive style. But they can help keep hair in place when you're setting it into a style by blow drying or using curling combs or tongs.

There are so many styling gels, mousses, sprays, pots and potions in the shops you'd think people spent all day layering them on. Some may, I suppose. The truth is that overdoing it can weigh down and dull your hair, so you shouldn't use too much of them.

The aim of styling aids, apart from protecting your hair from the drying effects of heat from a dryer, is to act as a light glue to 'stick' your hair into position, so you can see why you wouldn't want more than a dab (unless you're going for a punk look!). And you don't need one that contains conditioners (you already did that, remember?). Choose one that suits your hair.

GREASY OR NORMAL HAIR:

A gel works best on greasier or normal hair as it has a drying effect. It's got the strongest hold for gravity-defying styles!

NORMAL OR FLAKY HAIR:

A spray gives less of a drying effect, if your hair is normal or gets flaky.

FINE AND DRY HAIR:

A styling mousse will also help your hair to look thicker. Some contain moisturising ingredients as mousse can make your hair a bit dry – but the moisturising ingredients give the mousse less hold and can make your hair greasier quicker.

GET *stylish*

Now make sure you've got the styling aid spread evenly over your hair:

1 Use that fifty pence piece amount again for a gel or a tangerine-sized amount of mousse. Reduce the amount a bit for fine or shorter hair. Use more for longer and thicker hair.

2 Blob small bits on your fingertips, then dab it in areas at the roots. If you're using a spray, spray at the roots all over your head, lifting some sections to get at under hair at the back and sides.

3 Comb your hair through to distribute it evenly to the ends.

4 Now you're ready to blow dry your hair. If you simply want some bounce, tip your head upside down and aim the dryer at your roots. Move the dryer all the time so you don't get hot spots (and a sore scalp) in one area.

Be careful not to get longer hair sucked into the vent at the other end of the dryer (it can be very nasty for the style, not to mention painful for you and damaging to your hair!).

If you want a few waves, curls or direction, get sections of hair on a rounded brush into the right position (your hairdresser can show you). Point the dryer downwards from the roots along to the ends. If you aim the dryer upwards the tiny overlapping cuticles on each hair will be ruffled. When they stand up like this your hair looks fluffy and duller.

Which brush to use:

A small round brush gives tighter curls.

A semi circular one is better for creating bounce rather than waves.

A natural bristle brush grips the hair better than a synthetic one. Some hairdressers prefer not to use them as they can pull and break wet hair that is more elastic and weaker when wet. Use them with strong hair only when you need more grip for styling.

A round tipped brush is good for brushing wet hair or sore scalps as the protected spikes don't tear and damage so easily.

About hairdryers:

Many come with attachments:

A flattened nozzle, which attaches to a dryer, will channel the hot air for more concentration and precision on a specific area when drying.

A diffuser (the circular attachment with rounded spikes in them) is for laying large areas of your hair on. The dryer then helps dry your hair into a natural scrunchy waved look. It's especially good to bounce up already wavy hair. It is best to use a diffuser with a low heat setting on your dryer so as not to scald or dry your hair too much.

QUICK FIX

how to change your hair with some help from the experts

The fastest fix for hair you hate is to get a good haircut – one that can be easily styled to suit you and your hair type. Now by a good haircut I don't necessarily mean shorter. I'm talking about shaping and styling. You may even need to let it grow a bit to get the best style, but you should take some careful steps to make sure you get it.

A CLEVER HAIRDRESSER

A clever hairdresser can redesign your hair to make the most of what you have naturally. Hairdressers are trained to work with your natural hair. For instance, they'll take any kinks to make them fall like waves or change that annoying twist into something stylish.

A good hairdresser can cut a style to fall into place when you wash it and back into shape when you shake your head. It sounds like magic, right? How do you find the magician?

Making HEADWAY

The best way to find him or her is to ask people whose hair you admire where they had it done. Trust me, they'll be flattered. Then you need to analyse your own hair.

1 Is it: fine; thick; wavy; curly; frizzy; straight; greasy; dry; spiky? Add other things to describe it.

2 Now look at your face shape. Is it: round; square; thin; long; heart-shaped? etc.

3 Next comes the creative bit. Scan through magazines to find pictures of people with a similar hair type and face shape to yours. Think about whether you'd like their kind of hair-style. Cut out and keep those that you like. That's the kind of look that you're aiming for!

4 Then you can arrange a consultation with the hairdresser that you've found out about. Take these pictures along to the hair salon.

About Hair Salons

Almost all hair salons will give you a free consultation to discuss what you'd like and what they think will suit you.

You should show them your pictures and discuss your dreams for your hair. Don't set your heart on *exactly* the same look as your pictures. Your hair may not be the same thickness or degree of curl, or your face shape may be a bit different. The pictures will give your hair-stylist some idea of what you want. Remember to talk about your lifestyle with them. For instance, if you swim a lot, you wouldn't want a style that takes ten minutes to do each time it gets wet. Perhaps there's an alternative? For example, longer hair can be kept in a band or shorter hair slicked back for most of the week and be styled with a dryer for special occasions.

You'll need to return to the hairdressers every so often to keep your hair in shape. This is something to discuss at the consultation stage. Can you (or whoever is paying) afford regular trims every six weeks for a sharp cut? Or perhaps you should go for a softer or shaggier style that can grow happily for months on end before another cut? Many hairdressers have student discounts (that's for you) or student evenings (where student hairdressers practise on models) at little or no charge and under supervision from trained hairdressers.

You don't have to book an appointment after your consultation (although they'll hope you will). In fact, if it's a big change it's usually best to go away and think about it for a while to make sure it's what you really want. They won't be surprised if you do. If you're not sure, go to another recommended salon with your pictures and ask them what they could do. You shouldn't feel pressurised. After all it is your hair. A good stylist wouldn't want to give you a style that you didn't feel happy with – even if s/he thought you'd look amazing.

A good hairdresser can work wonders and make you look lovely – but they can't work miracles. They can't make curly hair permanently straight or straight hair into permanent waves (without a lot of regular technical treatments which can weaken the hair and cost more than a week's holiday each time). They can't make fine hair thicker (without a technical treatment, called extensions, at the cost of two weeks' holiday!).

Hair raising

Now a word of warning. It is wise to take along a parent, sister, brother or friend when you're first having your hair styled. There are a few odd stylists who get carried away with their own creativeness and forget about the person under their hair creation. Even those of us who know about hairdressing and have been going to salons for a few years get tongue–tied when our heads are in someone else's hands. A. N. Other can watch and can make sure the hairdresser doesn't cut off an extra inch or give you something like short sideburns or a fringe that you don't want. And they can back you up when you say STOP! And when you say stop, make sure they know you mean it. It's your head and your life and you have to live with it, in it. To be sure, you could ask the hairdresser to show you how much they're cutting off before they start.

A stylist who doesn't listen or do what you agreed is not a good hairdresser. They are not doing what they were trained to do, however talented they may be. Get up and leave if they're not listening. After all, even leaving with wet hair is better than living with a cut you hate until it grows out.

TROUBLE–SHOOTING

Q: Why does my hair look fine some days but makes me feel sick when I look in the mirror on others? Is this what's called a bad hair day?

A: Yes and everyone gets them – ask an honest adult. Your dad for instance. Perhaps you've even noticed his bad hair days? My dog certainly suffers from them (but she doesn't seem to care!). It can be caused by anything from static electricity in very dry atmospheres and the way you slept on your hair to what you've been eating (a change in your usual diet can make your hair and skin greasier). It may even be caused by washing your hair in a different water source. Softer or harder water can affect the pH balance of your hair which makes it silkier or drier. Perhaps you've noticed the change on holidays? Sometimes it's hormones (everyone has them, even the boys) taking a soar or dive and affecting the skin on your scalp. I'd advise trying to conceal difficult hair by using some of our natural foods in the Heady Stuff section to counteract whatever the problem is. Otherwise, take advantage of the situation to try a new style with some plaited or woven looks, bands, slides or hair slides.

slides

big plait

big band wrapped round

small plaits

band – with hair tucked in

Q: My hair is terminally frizzy. Help!

A: Okay, here's help. Frizzy hair is either naturally dry or temporarily very dry. I've never come across greasy frizzy hair as the greasiness controls the frizz. Both kinds of frizzy hair need plenty of conditioning to smooth it down and make it look glossier. Try regular long conditioning sessions, loading plenty of conditioner on your hair under a cling film turban (there it is again!). Keep it on for as long as you can stand before washing. Also stop blow drying or using heated appliances after every wash as they dry hair out more. Let your hair dry naturally sometimes. Use some of those serums or oils, that we talked about earlier, to smooth down the outer layer. For special occasions using heated curling tongs on well conditioned frizzy hair can help smooth it down into a more sleek style.

Q: I'm suffering from split ends. Is there a cure?

A: I'm afraid the only one is to cut them off! All hair is dead and split ends won't be repaired once they're there. You just have to wait until they grow long enough to trim. You can disguise them temporarily with a serum, as mentioned before, which sticks them together so they don't show so much. But this will wash or wear off. The secret is to avoid getting them again. Things that cause split ends are harsh handling, like pulling a brush through tangled hair, especially when it's wet, or using rubber bands to tie hair back (use a covered scrunchy type which won't pull so much). Chewing, twisting or overdrying hair in the sun or with a styler can also cause damage and fray the ends.

Q: I really, really want dark glossy hair. But I've got yucky mousy hair. Can I dye it?

A: You don't need to go that far! You can actually make hair a bit darker easily with conditioning wash-in colours that fade over six to eight shampoos. These don't do healthy hair any damage. But they won't change your hair dramatically as they're not permanent. Natural Henna (for red or darker hair) and Camomile (to brighten fairer hair) do the same. If you do decide to go for a tint of, say auburn, please read the instructions carefully first. Follow them to the letter. Especially the timing or you could end up with a bright orange shade! And please also ask your mum if it's okay first. I don't want her writing to me.

What you *can't* do is go lighter with these. To lighten or change hair colour dramatically, you need to alter the hair's chemical structure inside. And it's permanent until you cut it off, or it grows out. This leads to all sorts of problems if it's not done expertly, like damaging the hair so it breaks easily. Also if you look at your hair it's not just one single shade, it's many different strands of colour. In what you call mouse, you'll find hair of dark brown to pale blonde. One overall colour can look unnatural, and this is what permanent colourants do – give you block colour. Semi-permanents or temporary colours let your own natural variations show through. Also as hair grows from the roots, your natural colour shows through here in just a few weeks. With permanent colour the roots show quicker. Permanent colouring is really for people who are prepared to spend lots of time and effort on their hair and are absolutely sure that's the shade they want to stay. So stick to something easier that you can change if you want. Permanent colourants always have two bottles to mix. If you buy one like this by mistake, don't use it!

By the way, do you know that hairdressers say there isn't such a shade as mouse? It's classified as anything from fair or dark blonde to mid-brown.

Q: I am cursed with the dullest hair going! How can I get a super shine?
A: Not easy this one! The bottom line is that you can usually improve on what you're born with but only to a certain extent. Shine is caused by light reflecting on a smooth surface, so straight hair has the advantage for more light reflecting surface. If you've curly hair make it as smooth as possible by sticking down those hair tiles, that we talked about earlier, with good conditioning and serums.

Q: I'm ashamed to go out! The hairdresser gave me a horrible haircut yesterday. She said it looked good but I can tell everyone is laughing at me!
A: No time to lose then! Even hairdressers can have their off days. Go back to the salon with your mum, or someone who can back you up, and tell the manager you're really upset with it. A good salon won't be cross or angry but really will want you to be pleased with your style. And most will offer to do it again free. But you must give them a clear idea of what you want (see earlier in this chapter). If they've cut off too much it may mean reshaping it and letting it grow until you go back to them.

By the way, some styles do take time to get used to and you may find you like it after a week or so. And have you tried washing it? It may just be the blow dry you don't like. The cut may be fine. If the salon won't do anything about it, write it down to experience. Tell people not to go there and be determined to make sure the hairdresser does what you want next time.

Q: I'd like to weave my long hair but don't know how to do it.
A: It's not easy to describe but here goes! It's easier for someone to do it for you. For one woven plait like a cornrow running from your crown to nape (middle back) of your neck (see illustrations):

1. Make a parting from the top of one ear round over your crown to the top of the other ear.

2. Take the front bit and divide it into three equal sections from the sides of your forehead backwards to the parting. Leave the back hair hanging.

3. Plait the outside right strand of this section into the middle, then the left strand into the middle.

4. Holding on to these, take another section of hair from the top of the hanging bit at the back, just under the top of your right ear to the middle of the back of your head and add it to the strand of plait now situated on the right. Do the same with the left side.

5. Now weave both outside sections into the plait again. Repeat the process, adding sections of the hanging hair down your head in turn into the outside strands between plaiting, until all the hair is used up in the plait. Continue weaving the loose strands to the ends.

Having plaits and weaves, especially tight ones, can pull and break the hair – so try only to keep them in for a day at a time. And remember to use covered bands on the ends to prevent breaking.

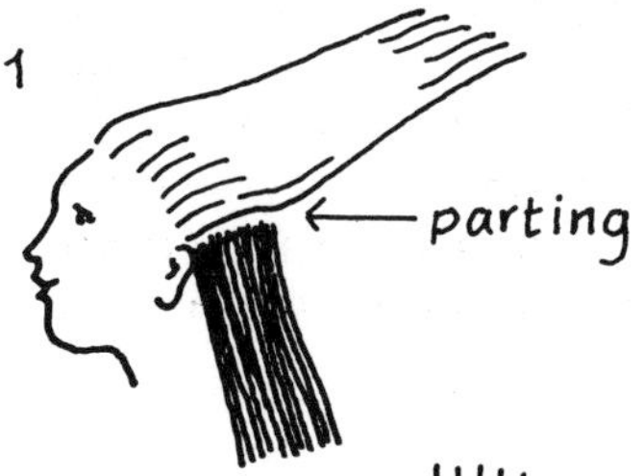

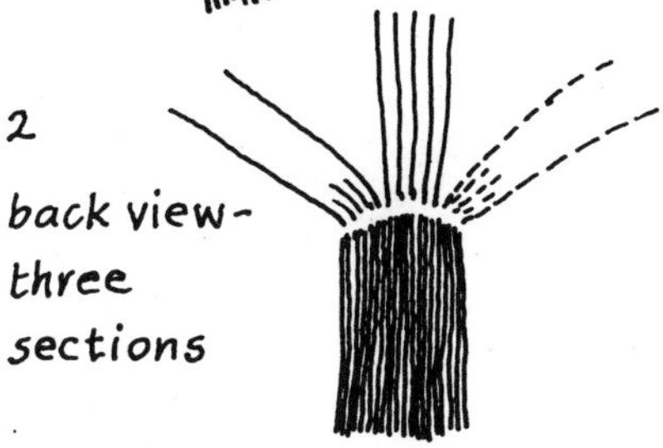

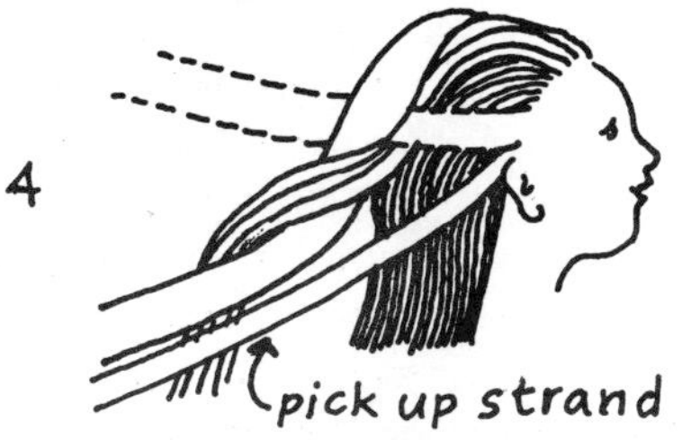

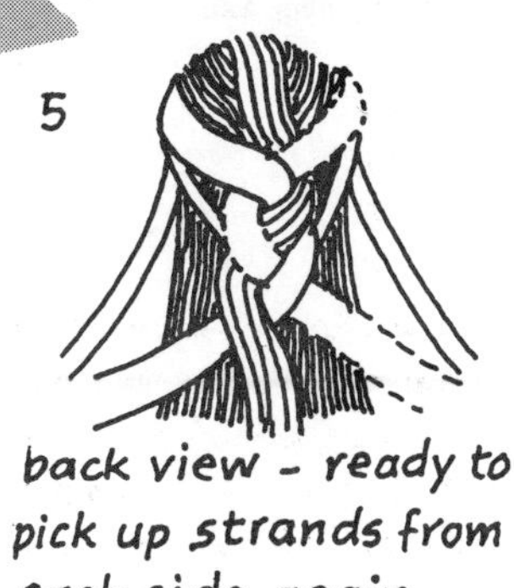

Q: Can you catch dandruff?

A: Definitely not! Even though it doesn't look nice, you can't catch it! A flaky scalp can be from not rinsing shampoo off properly, flaky setting products, a dry scalp or damage from brushing too hard. True dandruff is due to the microbe, Pityrosporum Ovale, going wild and causing natural skin shedding to speed up and drop off in clumps. P Ovale usually lives quite happily on our scalps (yes, everybody's!) and only tends to go mad when you've been ill, have an allergy, have unbalanced hormones (as you have during puberty) or are eating a bad diet. Ask your chemist for a good treatment shampoo. They take around three weeks of regular use to work.

Occasionally dandruff is due to a condition like psoriasis or eczema and you should see your doctor for treatment.

Q: I'm worried. There's always hair left on my brush after brushing it in the morning.

A: Don't worry, you're not going bald – it's completely normal. You shed about 80 hairs a day (meanwhile 80 new ones start to grow). At night the old ones don't get a chance to drop off naturally so they come out when you brush your hair first thing.

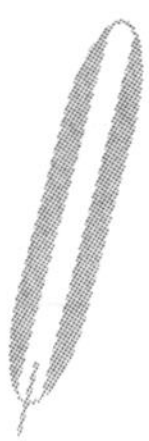

Chapter two

Skin Sense

you can amaze and astound others with them

Here are some facts and figures to amaze and astound you! If you like, you can amaze and astound others with them later.

Your skin, yes yours, covers around four and a half square metres (five in adult men) and weighs about two and a half kilograms (seven to eight in adult men).

It's the body's largest organ and completely renews itself every twenty-eight days.

It's waterproof on the outside (so those ball point marks don't reach your inside). But it keeps you together and hardly lets anything out unless you damage it. Normally all that escapes is moisture and body waste products (sweat) plus some natural oils.

Sweating and shivering help keep your body temperature even so that you don't boil or freeze. And talking of sweating, we perspire between one and ten, sometimes up to twenty, pints every day! Not all at once, you understand, but it feels like it sometimes, like before exams for instance. Usually it's just slowly evaporating as we go about doing what we have to do. But in hot weather or when you're nervous, even when you eat curry, you sweat much more. As your skin is around 80 per cent water (less as you get older) it's important to drink lots of water at these time to prevent you looking like a prune!

Skin makes antibacterial oils (sebum) as a protective cover and moisturiser to fight germs and allow your skin to be flexible and to bend.

In fact, skin is more elastic than rubber – that's why people who lose lots of weight don't have folds hanging off them! It just springs back.

pinch it and see!

Even the cleverest scientist couldn't have designed a better packaging for us. Skin looks good (or we humans tend to think so) and also helps you make contact by touching. So it warns you about danger with hot or sharp objects and gives you pleasure with things like stroking a cat or swimming in warm water.

What's YOUR Skin type?

So soft, glowing skin makes you look great and helps to keep you healthy. If you want, you can secretly blame any skin problems on your parents as you inherit from them a certain skin type. Other problems are due to environment: you're more likely to get allergies and spots in polluted, dusty or centrally heated places. Then there's your age. The hormones that are buzzing around changing your body, also affect your skin. You're more likely to get spots, some allergies and greasiness as you start getting curves. These aren't things you can change but you do grow out of them. You can treat most problems to make your skin better.

Greasy Skin

TEENAGERS ARE ESPECIALLY LIKELY TO HAVE GREASY SKIN.
IT PRODUCES MORE NATURAL OILS, SO HAS A SHINY APPEARANCE AND IS MORE LIKELY TO GET SPOTS.
IT'S IMPORTANT TO CLEAN IT THOROUGHLY AND REGULARLY TO STOP EXCESS OIL CLOGGING PORES AND GIVING YOU SPOTS.

Dry Skin

This feels tight and can look dull as the drier top skin gives a grey look. It may even flake off sometimes.
Dry skin needs regular cleaning to remove top dry skin cells and a good dose of moisturiser regularly to keep it supple and protected from getting drier.

Combination Skin

This has greasy and dry or normal patches. Each area should be treated according to its skin type.

Sensitive Skin

This quickly reacts to outside influences like heat, cold, harsh handling or allergens with rashes, broken veins, itching and dryness.
It needs to be treated gently. Stick to unperfumed skin care and steer clear of exfoliators (see later in the chapter).

By looking after your skin you can stop some problems happening or improve those that have happened. Looking after means cleansing and moisturising. It should take five minutes maximum, morning and evening.

You may think that your skin is all one piece, but it's not. New skin cells constantly form deep down. They slowly rise to the surface bonded together, linger for a while, then dry up and drop off.

CLEAN SWEEPS

Your skin grows faster at night so cleansing in the morning takes off the top dead skin cells which have accumulated as you sleep. Cleansing at night wipes away the day's dirt and grime, so your skin looks pinker and brighter.

Water isn't enough to dissolve the stale natural oils (which hold dirt). Soap is too acidic and destroys the delicate pH balance (acid/alkali ratio – ask your chemistry teacher!) of the skin's natural protective cover, so regularly using soap can make your face look like a full time dishwasher's hands! Gently massage cleanser on with your fingertip pads (those are soft bits), and then wipe it off with tissue.

Toners or toning lotion bought in the shops, are designed to freshen you up and remove all the greasiness left on your face from the cleanser. Follow cleansing by wiping your face with toning lotion on a tissue or cotton wool. If the cleanser says you can rinse it off with water, water can act as a toner instead on normal skin.

Normal or dry skin

Try a water and oil mix such as a shop bought cleanser or baby lotion (not baby oil) on normal and dry skin.
If your skin is dry, wipe it off with a tissue or cotton wool (mind those fibres in your eyes).

Greasier skins

Use a lotion cleanser that can be washed off if you've got greasier skin. Blot it with cotton wool soaked in a toner afterwards. Thin slices of cucumber can act as a toner for greasy skin.
For all skins, but particularly effective on greasy ones you can use a specially designed wash-off cleanser instead.
These are usually in a tube and have added lather but sometimes look like a bar of soap which doesn't lather much (because it's pH balanced to your skin – ask your teacher).

Combination skin

If some areas of your face are dry and some greasy, treat each area according to its type.

Sensitive skin

Now, according to the skin care manufacturers, people like pretty smells in their cleansers. Personally I don't see the point of putting perfumed cleanser on your face, because you wipe it off straight away, and it is more likely to cause a skin reaction. If you have sensitive skin you should use an unfragranced cleanser. They're sometimes called 'hypoallergenic' or – stating the obvious – 'unperfumed'.

For deep cleansing try milk (yes, Cleopatra had the right idea). But make sure you get rid of the traces – stale milk does *not* smell nice! Rinse it off well with splashes of water.

EYE MAKE-UP REMOVERS

These are greasier to dissolve stubborn make-up more gently. You'd really only need them for waterproof mascara. Gently dab and wipe them off with a tissue.

FACE MASKS

These take more time as they're left on for ten to twenty minutes and are heavy duty treatments to deep clean or moisturise skin when it's particularly dull or dry. Gritty cleansing ones, like mud, have a polishing effect (like sandpaper but hopefully not so rough) to remove top dead layers of skin cells. Don't use these more than once a week.

EXFOLIATORS

These can be like sandpaper! They often contain particles to buff away top skin cells, which make skin look dull. Underneath a pinker layer of skin is revealed. Younger skins don't need them. If you've got really dull skin, a damp, rough flannel will work just as well. Fruit acid, or Aha's, found in some cleansers and skin creams, are chemical exfoliators which dissolve the bonds between surface skin cells so they drop off. They are for older skins which don't renew so fast. You don't need them.

SKINNY dipping

Moisturising your face adds water to the surface layers to top up what's already there and keep it bouncy. The oil content then helps to seal it all in. Find a light moisturiser. These are usually the most liquid ones that sink in quickly. Stroke on a five pence sized blob after you've cleansed and toned. Do it more often, like midday as well, if you've dry skin. Use an even lighter, more liquid one if you have greasy or spotty skin.

Haven't got any moisturiser and can't beg, borrow or steal some? If you've normal or dry skin, try baby lotion, again. No tiny brothers or sisters? Then try the smallest dot of cooking oil rubbed over your palms first then patted on. At a pinch use margarine, suncream or unfragranced body lotion. But, beware: all these can be too rich and clogging for skin prone to greasiness and spots.

GOING FOR GOLD

I don't think I know anyone who hasn't done this at least once:

The sun is out and you are as free as a bird. You can't wait to get outside. You forget about all the winter gloom and spend the best day ever, wearing as little as is decent, in the great outdoors. But here comes the hard part. By evening you have a face that could pass for a stop sign and a perfect white print on your body showing exactly where those clothes have been. If you're lucky you spend the next few days with bits of skin dropping off your nose. If you're unlucky, it comes off in great strips, revealing pale pink skin underneath which is sore as well. It's not a pretty sight!

Skin specialists would rather we didn't sunbathe. They say it's the worst thing we can do to our skin. They say regularly suntanned skin ages faster, making us look twenty years older at forty. You may not think that's a big deal now. But ask a forty-year-old how she'd like to look sixty (then quickly tell her she looks thirty!). **You'll see the point!**

Sunbathing, the doctors say, can cause some nasty problems in the longer term, apart from ageing faster. That's because sunlight can damage the 'blueprint' which helps make new skin cells deep in the skin. So new skin cells become deformed. Sounds horrible, doesn't it? But that's what they say and they should know – they've spent a lot of time researching it. So take that into consideration.

The good news is that an even, golden tan makes you feel great! It gives your skin a wonderful glow and makes your eyes and teeth look whiter and healthier. And sunlight helps to manufacture Vitamin D in the body. That's the one that promotes stronger nails and bones and gives skin and hair better condition.

So with this conflicting information, what should you do? Stay pale and be as fashionable as some top models who never sunbathe? Or compromise to get a light tan? The compromise is to tan really slowly with sunscreen. It takes longer but the tan will last longer. There'll be no piebald effect and it's the safest way to do it. It makes more sense if you know how it works:

AS SIMPLE AS abc

The sun throws off many rays, including light rays. The particular ones that tan you are called ultra violet light. Tanning ultra violet (or UV) light is broken down into different strengths – ultra violet A (UVA), UVB and UVC. In reverse order:

UVC

is almost all dispersed by the ozone layer before it reaches the earth. Only high mountain climbers, air pilots or astronauts in their aeroplanes or rockets really have to worry about this ferocious burning light. That's unless we damage the ozone layer too much, of course!
Then UVC will get through and we, animals and plants are all in big trouble!

UVB

is the main one that everyone talks about in suntanning. It's the burning ray that starts your skin stinging in seconds if you've got pale skin. It will burn you before it tans you.

UVA is the main one used in sunbeds. That's because it tans you first but takes a longer time to burn you. Now you may think that this sounds okay. You'll save up and go for some tanning without burning sessions. Think again! It's been found that UVA actually goes deeper into your skin. So, without warning, it can cause havoc which may not show up until years later (remember the forty-year-old!). Most sunscreens (sun creams, gels, sprays and lotions) now screen against UVB and UVA.

Joining the brownies

Our wonderful skins produce a natural pigment (or colouring) when the sun shines on them. It's called melanin. Black people are born with lots already in their skin. Pale skins have very little. When your skin meets sunlight it says to itself 'Help, I need protecting from burning'. Then it starts producing more melanin to block the sun and stop your insides frying. The trouble is, it can only go so far. Hit with strong sunlight for a while most white skin starts burning before it gets a chance to make the barrier. So the secret to a good suntan is to do it gradually, to help push melanin into production, without burning and doing deeper damage. The way to do this is to allow only little amounts of sunlight to get to your skin at a time. And the easy way to do this is with sunscreen. Without sunscreen you'd be popping inside and outside all the time to get a safe tan.

The sunscreens in the shops show their strengths with numbers. The higher the Sun Protection Factor (SPF) number, the more it screens your skin from the sun. Numbers go from 2 to around 30 but most are from 4 to 15.

So how do you know which you need? Good question! First look at your skin type.

Do you have:

Very fair skin, with red, white blonde or black hair, green or pale blue eyes? Does your skin almost always burn as soon as it sees the sun? This is bad news for suntanning I'm afraid. Your skin is very delicate and the most easily damaged by sunlight. Most very fair skin just doesn't have enough melanin producing cells to give it a tan. That means you'd only burn. If this is you, say to yourself that you'll be different from the crowd. You'll stay pale and interesting. But that doesn't mean you can't go out! You can put on a sun barrier. These are simply called sunblocks or have an SPF of between 15 and 30. I'd go for the highest you can find, to be sure not to burn. When they're put on properly and regularly, sunblocks should stop the sun from reaching your skin completely. You'd also be wise to cover up with T-shirts and big hats.

Sorry about THAT!

Fair skin,

prone to allergy and irritation, with fair or dark hair and light eyes? Does it burn easily in the sun – say within ten to fifteen minutes? Remember this number for later.

Normal skin,

which never really looks pale in the winter but can burn after thirty minutes or so in hot sun?

Yellow toned skin,

the so-called Mediterranean type because it's normal in places like Spain, Greece, Southern France, Italy? It tans easily but can burn if you're out for an hour or so.

Black skin,

which only burns in long bouts of strong sunlight?

You may be in between two of these. If you've been unlucky enough to have burnt already try to remember (or ask your mum) how long it took and how strong the sun was so you can take that into the equation below.

How's your maths?

You'll need it for this bit:

1. Work out, from your skin type (above) how long you could stay in hot sunlight without burning (let's say it's fifteen minutes).

2. Then work out how long you want to stay in the sun (how about three hours or 180 minutes?).

3. Now divide your skin type time (fifteen) into your sunbathing time in minutes (180) to get the sun protection factor (SPF) you need (in this case it would be 180 divided by 15 = 12).

4. That's the number you choose on your sun cream or lotion. (So, with our example, it would be SPF 12.)

Have you got the sun protection equation? If you have normal skin which you estimate will burn after thirty minutes without protection and you want to sunbathe for an hour (sixty minutes) an SPF 2 (sixty

divided by thirty) sunscreen should be all you need. Darker skin, which won't burn for forty-five minutes, can be in the sun all morning without burning if it's covered with an SPF 5 **(5 x 45 = 225 minutes or 3 hours 45 minutes).**

Did you know that you can burn through cloud on hazy days and through some glass? Also up to three feet under water? Wear sunscreen when the sun shines.

In addition: you will gradually tan through a sunscreen. But there are some extra things to watch for:

Around midday, on higher ground (up a mountain) or nearer the equator, the earth is nearer to the sun (ask your geography teacher). Rays are more intense and stronger. Your skin type 'burn time' will be lower and so you'll need a higher SPF number on your sunscreen.

Shaving or waxing your legs takes off the very top (dead) layer of skin. New skin is more vulnerable. Skin is also new where you've scraped it or have scars and so it's more likely to burn here. You need a higher SPF than normal on these areas.

If you go in the water, use a water resistant sunscreen. But don't expect miracles from it. Lots of splashing, vigorous swimming or playing watersports will wear it off. And it won't stay on if you towel dry yourself. Reapply sunscreen often and after swimming. Heavy sweating will also dilute sunscreen.

KEEP TOPPING IT UP.

Light reflects off some surfaces. Snow, water, sand, white walls and pale paving stones are just some that you have to watch for. You'll be getting more than your fair share when you're near these. The rays will be more intense and stronger on your skin. Wear a higher SPF screen number.

If you use perfumed skin care, like moisturiser, deodorants and soaps, they can react with sunlight. This causes skin sensitivity and a rash or pigment patching. Use a sunblock or remember to wash with unfragranced soap or cleanser before putting on suncream.

Some drugs, like antibiotics, and hormonal disturbances (the pill, pregnancy) can cause darker pigment patches in the sun. They usually fade with the tan. If your doctor prescribes medication before going on holiday, ask whether it's likely to cause this reaction and use a sunblock if you don't want to risk it.

If you're unsure of which number to go for, err on the side of caution and choose a <u>HIGHER</u>, rather than lower, number.

picking your PROTECTOR

Now you've worked out your own individual **SPF**, decide which type of sunscreen to get:

DRY SKIN

Creams are the heaviest and best for dry skin. They moisturise and can carry the highest sunscreen. Most sunblocks are in cream form.

ALL SKIN TYPES

Lotions (also called milks) are thinner and the most popular type. They're for all skin types and can carry lots of SPF if needed. But they're more likely than any to wear off easily with friction, sweat or water.

GREASY OR SPOTTY SKIN

Gels are good for those with greasy, problem or sweaty skin. They leave a fine film on the skin which feels dry. If you hate the slippery feel of creams and lotions, are worried about oiliness marking clothes or want to put make-up over the top, get a gel.

SPRAYS

These work well for people who hate any kind of lotion on their skin. But you need to make sure you spray them evenly to cover every bit of skin in the sun. For your face, spray on to your palms. Lightly rub them together and then pat it on to your face.

SENSITIVE SKIN

If you suffer from allergies choose a hypoallergenic range or look at the small print. Avoid the ones that have chemical sunscreens in them, like oxybenzone and methoxycinnamate, which sink in and react with your skin to protect you. Instead, find a sunscreen that acts as a barrier. You can't see them but those with mica or titanium dioxide in them have tiny particles which lie on top of your skin. Look for these names on the bottle if you have sensitive skin.

Sunblocks are good for when you've used up your sunscreen time and want to stay on the beach, or go for a swim or do whatever in the sun. Slap them on in a good, even layer and carry on without worrying about burning.

COUNT DOWN TO SUN

Put your sunscreen on to dry skin before you go out. Make sure it's in an even layer. Reapply every hour or immediately after swimming. Aim to turn a flattering gold shade rather than a deep bronze, which doesn't look so good on white skin. Then say goodbye to all that horrible shiny redness and flaking skin! And hello to a beautiful even glow!

Brown FROM A Bottle

This is what the skin doctors would like us to do for a tan.

FAKE IT! FAKE IT! FAKE IT! FAKE IT! FAKE IT! FAKE IT!

Self tan has an ingredient (DHA) which was discovered in men's shaving lotions. Men kept turning brown – but in patches! Now you can find ones that work like a treat to give you a golden brown colour if you use them properly.

Fake or self tans develop slowly in a couple of hours to a permanent brown shade, then gradually fade away over a week or so. And they're completely safe. Well, to your health anyway. Some people have got the most terrible looking streaks from them.

There is definitely some working out and planning here, too. But it's worth it for brown legs or filling in those white swimsuit strap marks.

First choose the right one:

Normal and dry skins

Moisturised ones (creams and lotions) are best for normal skins. I'd recommend the very light ones (usually they're for faces but you can use them anywhere). As they don't give such a dark shade you can make sure that the results are even first (it won't be so obvious if it's a bit streaky) then do it again if you want the full blown two week holiday away look!

Greasier skins

Gels and sprays are for the experts and those with oilier skins. They sink in quicker and give you less rubbing in time.

Now prepare to bronze

1

Make sure there are no rough
patches so you've smooth skin
to put them on. This will
make the finished look more
even on your skin. Use a
rough flannel or loofah in the
bath or shower to gently rub
away any rough patches or
flakiness. Dry or rough skin
can cause uneven patching
with fake or self tans.

2

Moisturise the area you want to tan. Wait for at least thirty minutes afterwards to let it sink in.

3

Apply small blobs to the centre of the skin you want to tan. Now rub them in quickly and thoroughly so they join up. Fade it off towards the thicker skin areas (knees, heels, elbows) and the edges (top of legs, neck, hairline).

5

NOW WASH YOUR HANDS!

4

Keep rubbing it in evenly even if you can't see it, until all the lotion goes and it doesn't feel sticky. This is where many a streak has been created! People don't rub self tan in enough.

6

Don't let the areas you've treated come into contact with anything else for at least thirty minutes.

Happy bronzing!

Self tan works best on those with yellow toned skin (rather than pink toned).
But very fair skin can look glowing with a lighter cover.

THE Body *Beautiful*

Although it's covered most of the year, the rest of your skin could do with a bit of attention sometimes, too. Especially when it's most at risk from getting dry. That's after sunbathing, in drying atmospheres (central heating, cold dry days and wind) and when you've been ill.

The best conditioner is drinking pure water – lots of it; at least a pint a day with other liquids like tea and juice. Second best is any liquid drinks but steer clear of too many fizzy cola-types, sugary fruit juices or fatty ones, like milk shakes.

✪ You should also put water on your skin and then seal it there with moisturiser. Just like your face. You can do this easily on your body with oils in your bath. Just add a few drops to the water – not too much or you'll need another bath! When you emerge, they'll leave a very fine layer of oil on your skin.

Pat yourself dry so as not to rub it off. By the way, you're duty bound to wash the bath afterwards – this will leave a ring in the tub!

✪ After-sun lotions and creams have special soothing ingredients to calm sun-sore skin down. Pat it on after a warm (not hot) bath or shower. It'll moisturise your skin, too.

✪ Body milks and lotions act as moisturisers for body skin. *Now's* the time to get one with a sensational smell, too, but avoid the fragranced ones if you've got sensitive skin.

Feeding *your* Skin

How about going back to the larder again? But this time for your skin. Remember not to let anyone go hungry in the process!

FOR SMOOTHER SKIN

Who can afford the milk for a Cleopatra-type bath? You can, if you borrow some dried milk granules. Add a cupful to warm water. Mix them in. Now soak!

FOR FLAKY SKIN OR PATCHES OF OLD SELF TAN

These can be removed by rubbing salt (any will do but coarse salt, as used for dishwashers, is best) or oatmeal gently over wet skin. Massage it on in a circular movement. Rinse well, then moisturise.

FOR MOISTURISING

Cooking oil, such as sunflower, can double up as bath oil – just a few drops remember!

FOR RELAXING

Make a small pouch from some old tights. This is to hold your additives as they soak in the water. It'll stop getting bits floating all over you and down the plughole. Fill it with some dried lavender or rose petals from the garden or marjoram from the herb rack. Put the pouch in the warm water and let it soak away your troubles. Or try a camomile tea bag in the water.

FOR AN INVIGORATING BATH

Make the same pouch and add some (clean) pine needles from the garden or rosemary from the herb rack. Or add some fresh lime or lemon juice. Alternatively, try a peppermint tea bag in the water to pep you up.

Skin treatments

CLEANING GRIMY SKIN

Massage into dry skin a tablespoon of liquid honey or wheatgerm. Rinse it off thoroughly with warm water.

TONING

Add a teaspoon of cider vinegar or witchhazel to half a cup of water. Soak a piece of cotton wool or tissue and dab it on to your skin to remove oiliness.

SPOTS

Draw them out with an onion baked in the oven. Put it over the spot when it's as hot as you can bear it but not scalding – test it on your hand first.

MOISTURISING

Try an egg yolk, mashed banana or a teaspoon of mayonnaise patted on to your skin for fifteen minutes while you relax. Rinse it off well.

PROBLEM SKIN

A tablespoon of live yoghurt can cleanse, moisturise and fight bacteria. Massage it on gently with clean fingertips. Leave it there for a few minutes and wipe it off with a tissue.

GREASY SKIN

Try a lightly whisked egg white for fifteen minutes to absorb the oiliness. Rinse it off and reapply every week.

SORE EYES

Slices of raw potato are better than cucumber for dry and normal skin to reduce any swelling and brighten them up. Lie down and place thin potato slices over each eye. Stay still for fifteen minutes.

Q: I've just started using beauty products like skin care and make-up, but I've broken out in an itchy red rash around my mouth. Can they have caused it?

A: Yes, they might have. It sounds like an allergy but what caused it is tricky to figure out.

You can actually be allergic to anything (even, in rare cases, water) but there are some things that are more likely to cause allergies. It could have been something you've eaten, pollution, stress or something you've had direct contact with such as detergent from the pillow you sleep on, hand cream, nail polish or shampoo, if you've long hair that covers your face. But as you've just started using beauty products I think you'd be right to investigate these first.

Try doing a patch test by dabbing some of each product on your inside arm near the elbow. Cover each of them with a plaster or bandage for twenty-four hours, then see if any react. If this doesn't work, stop using the things that are most likely to cause an allergy. These are:

* Anything fragranced (opt for unperfumed).
* Anything with preservatives (especially formaldehyde and alcohol – read the ingredients labelling).
* Anything containing pigments (especially red eosin, inorganic yellow, rust iron oxide – some are used to colour skin care as well as make-up). If there aren't any lists on the bottles, ask the place where you bought them to find out the ingrdients for you.

If this fails, stop using all your beauty products. If your allergy fades, start reusing them one by one until you find the culprit. And if you're still getting itchy skin, try a mild hydrocortisone cream from the chemist on your rash – your pharmacist will advise you on which one – or visit your doctor for further investigations.

Q: My face has areas that look like the surface of the moon. Where can I get big paper bags?

A: Take heart – very few escape the Great Spots War in their teens and most of us came through it with okay skin in the end. You feel they're bigger and more noticeable than they look. Everyone says this, so it must be true! Make sure you're cleansing and toning properly so you don't give the volcanoes more ammunition but weaken their defences. And fight back with some benzoyl peroxide lotion (ask your pharmacist again) on the exact area of each spot – going on to unaffected skin can make it flaky.

I *know* it's tempting, but do not squeeze them unless they're about to burst. Then do it carefully by soaking them with warm water on a clean flannel and gently pushing the sides with a tissue. Any force drives bacteria deeper into the skin and makes the eruption larger and last longer. It'll also immediately make the spots look more angry and red. A far better tactic is to work on some camouflage with a medicated concealer.

Look at the colour before you buy it and avoid the very orangy pinks – unless you've got very orangy pink skin, of course!

Now get artistic. Use a clean fine tipped brush to paint the concealer on to the area you need to cover, putting a thicker dab on the parts that show most. For larger areas try a cotton bud. Blend it into your skin at the edges. Hey presto! No paper bags needed!

Q: I loathe my freckles but they appear with the sun each summer. Is there any way to get rid of them?

A: Sorry! The only permanent method I know of is laser surgery by a specialised doctor, and I doubt whether any doctor would do it on freckles (disfiguring birthmarks and scars are another matter). Did you know that some cosmetic companies have actually brought out pencils for non-freckled people to use to paint them in? It's personal taste, I suppose.

One of the best ways to avoid sun-induced freckles is to use a sunblock but you won't get a tan, either. Otherwise use a concealer (non-medicated and as near your face skin colour as possible) in the way described above and paint them out. But don't go sunbathing after this either or you could end up with a very blotchy looking face!

Q: I always use sunscreen and I always burn, then peel. Why?

A: Do you use a high enough SPF? See above for advice. It's important not to burn in the sun. Not just because it's sore and peeling skin doesn't look attractive but because it damages your skin and leads to skin problems later. You are more likely to get wrinkles and skin cancer when you're older if you burn now. And if you burn, you'll peel. That's how the skin gets rid of useless covering. Use a soothing lotion such as calamine or a sun first aid spray to calm down the areas. Take tepid (not hot or cold) baths and showers. Drink plenty of water to help your skin recover. And if you feel dizzy, lie in a darkened room. If you still feel ill after twenty-four hours see a doctor. Until your skin is back to normal stay out of the sun – or cover up completely if you can't avoid it. Never sunbathe with peeling skin – you can do permanent damage. And remember that newly peeled skin is back to the palest it gets. Use a high protection SPF if you go in the sun again.

Q: What can I do about my hairy legs? Options please!

A: The person, and I suspect it may be a woman, who comes up with a permanent answer to defuzzing, will immediately be able to retire on the proceeds. Many have tried and failed. Okay, here are the options for leg, armpit and bikini line hair, with the pros and cons:

* Shaving is quick and easy using an electric or protected blade shaver specially made for the job. *But* hair grows back within a day or two and feels stubbly as it is cut off bluntly.

* Depilatory creams dissolve hair to just under the skin surface and last for up to a week. *But* they are messy, can be smelly and you have to hang around for up to twenty minutes waiting for them to work.

* Waxing and sugaring removes hair for up to three weeks as it pulls them out at the roots. *But* it's like ripping off a plaster, so can be painful, home kits and strips take skill to use effectively and going to a beautician takes time and money.

* You can get plug-in gadgets which look like electric shavers but actually aim to grip and pull out hair like waxing. *But* they often snap them off so act more like shavers and can be painful.

For individual hairs in the wrong place, electrolysis is where a skilled operator puts a fine needle into each hair shaft to send a low electrical current and zap the hair root. *But* it can be very painful, costly and time consuming. Although it's meant to be permanent, it usually takes a few sessions over months.

For most individual hairs for instance between your eyebrows, plucking with a tweezer is the easiest and best.

If you have heavy or dark hair hair over your top lip, you could try bleaching it with kits from the chemist or waxing as above.

Now the choice is yours!

Chapter three

Figuring it out

Do you know that even the most beautiful women in the world would like to change something about their appearance? Go on – ask someone who you think is perfect the one thing they'd change if they could. I'd bet you'll get more than one!

It's because we're all different in shape, size, colouring and personality that makes us attractive and interesting. If we all had the same perfect figures, life would be pretty boring, wouldn't it? And when it comes to boys, you'll find that they don't necessarily like the girls that you think are ideal. Often it's the one with the big nose or chubby thighs they go for (and like because of it). And you may find the boy with the sticking out ears or gangly figure is the one you'd most like to see more of. But the chances are, he's hoping he'll wake up one morning minus the noticeable ears and with a muscular physique.

"You can make the most of your own distinct appearance. Creating your own individual style will make you a uniquely attractive person and it will give you confidence and sparkle. In other words, it's worth any extra effort it takes."

"Balancing" acts!

As I have said, your appearance is individual to you. You may think your figure is too small, big, lopsided, fat, thin etc. But you'll also find that as you continue through life your body has its own agenda. It changes shape. So the shape you are now will almost certainly not be the same in a year or two and it will change again a few years after that. Your figure at twenty will be different again. And again at forty or sixty.

Nature does have something to do with keeping you in some sort of line. It has already decided your basic frame. That is, whether you'll be tall or short or inclined to be curvy or straight. The rest is down to you and your lifestyle. There's very little you can do to change nature, but lifestyle is a different matter. That's where the choices come in – lifestyle can make an okay figure great or not so good.

Aim for the best possible figure, improving on what nature has given you, with a good lifestyle. The way to dramatically improve your appearance is by eating and exercising properly and regularly.

But first some pure magic to make you look slimmer, taller and firmer in an instant:

a Firmer Trimmer figure in an instant

It's dead simple. Just try these four steps and see! All you need are a full length mirror and your birthday suit on. Clothes can hide any figure faults. But we'll come to how to use that to your advantage later!

1

Stand in front of the mirror with your feet about one metre apart and flat on the ground, facing forwards. Your hands should hang loosely at your sides.

2

Keeping your chin level (not up or down), stretch your neck up and your shoulders down. Feel as though a big weight is on your shoulders.

3

Now pull your stomach and bottom in, with your knees ever so slightly bent.

4

Imagine that a big thread is running through your middle from the centre of the floor between your feet to the top of your head and it's pulling you up.

It's called good posture!

Posture ++++++plus++

If you find it difficult to keep this position, a little more work with an exercise to do fifteen times a day will help. It tones up your muscles so you can hold better posture for longer; eventually you can hold your good slimmer shape all the time. You can do this exercise anywhere: at the bus stop, doing the ironing, watching TV. It's best not to have an audience though!

1 Stand in your usual position, sideways to the mirror (head turned to look at it though!).

2 Notice where your shoulders slope and bottom sticks out.

3 Pull your shoulders back and keep your neck and head in a normal position (so they don't feel strained).

4 Breathe in deeply, then out.

5 Scoop your bottom under, squeezing your behind together.

6 Holding that position, pull your stomach in.

7 Tense up in all those areas that you're holding in.

8 Hold for a count of three.

9 Relax and repeat it **fourteen MORE TIMES.**

FOOD *for* THOUGHT

Food and drink is the body's fuel, maintaining and repairing material.

What you eat will show up in how you look and feel. Put the right stuff in and you'll go far and look good while you're getting there. By putting the right stuff in I mean eating in a balanced way, not over or under eating – not for long periods anyway. There's no problem with going off food when you're ill for a few days or being a bit mad with the ice creams on holiday and chocolates at Christmas. But too much food over a length of time makes you blobby, wobbly and weary. Too little nourishment can make you look like a ghost, damage your health and you'll also look younger. Aim to eat regular healthy meals most of the time.

Good, sensible, regular eating will help you stay in top health and full of energy. It'll keep your skin, hair and nails in good condition and make your eyes shine.

A ROUGH GUIDE *to a* SENSIBLE DAY'S EATING

This is a sketchy idea of what and when you should be eating every day, rather than a precise health plan. You won't put on or lose weight and it's not especially geared to diets like vegetarian ones (although the options are there). It shows you the balance of nutrients you need to stay in tip top health.

Breakfast

A bowl of wholegrain
(oats, wheat etc) and
fruit (raisins, nuts etc.)
cereal with milk and
honey or two slices
of brown bread with butter
and jam/marmalade.
A glass of fruit juice or
piece of fruit.

Mid morning

Milk or milky drink and fruit bar or piece of fruit.

Lunch

Some mixed raw or lightly cooked vegetables or meat or fish with salad and/or vegetables and bread or potatoes. Fresh fruit with yoghurt or ice cream.

Mid afternoon

A fruity drink, tea or water with a small nutty bar.

Dinner

Vegetables, or white meat, or fish, with potatoes, pasta or rice and raw or lightly cooked vegetables or salad. Fresh fruit salad with yoghurt or crème fraiche or a fruity type pudding.

Mid evening

A milky drink and one wholemeal biscuit.

ACTION!

Exercise is the thing to help firm you up and form curves in the right places. We're not talking body building here, just regular activity to keep your muscles trim and hold them better on your frame, so you go in and out where you should.

Exercise also helps that fuel you've put in work better. It raises your *metabolism*. Your metabolism is your body's programming which helps it to function, and it affects everything – even the smallest body cell. By raising your metabolism everything works better.

Experts recommend exercising at least twenty to thirty minutes three times a week, so you can see it's not a full time occupation. Especially not for something that makes you look your best and gets your body to work super

efficiently.

Frame **firmers**

You've found out how to have the best posture and you need that befor start exercising. Bad posture won't allow you good flexibility to exercis can make you work muscles in the wrong way or damage them while y doing it. Here are some suggestions for that twenty minutes of exercise times a week.

Check with your doctor before doing any exercise if you've recently been ill or suffered from any breaks or sprains, and always warm up with a stretch (like the cat below) before starting any of the other groups of exercises.

Try to vary them so that you're not doing the same activity each time:

STRETCHING EXERCISES

These are good to tone you up and give you suppleness and stamina. You'll also find they can calm you down and make you feel more relaxed as you have to concentrate on them rather than other things. All stretches should be slow and gentle rather than jerky or bouncy.

Start off by stretching all over, like a cat. Start at the tips of your toes and work up to you ankles, calves, knees etc, stretching every part of your body. Even stretch those parts you wouldn't think you can stretch. Like your ears! Go on try it – you'll be surprised!

INNER THIGHS, CALVES AND OUTER LEGS, STOMACH AND BOTTOM:

1. Stand with your feet firmly on the ground a metre apart.
2. Turn your toes out as far as possible pointing away from each other. Your heels should be turned in, pointing towards each other (widen your feet a bit if you feel you might fall over!).
3. Keeping your knees pointed out, your shoulders back and stomach and bottom in, put your hands on your hips.
4. Now, keeping your bottom in, slowly start to sit, going down as far as you can.
5. Hold it for two seconds
7. Slowly come back up and go right up on to your toes, gently lifting your arms above your head without hunching your shoulders and stretching your neck up (shoulders down remember). *Feel like a ballerina? Then you're doing it properly!*

TO KEEP YOUR SHOULDERS BACK, BOTTOM UNDER AND TO STRENGTHEN THE FRONT OF YOUR LEGS:

1. Stand with your feet a metre apart again, your shoulders back and your stomach in.
2. Keeping your back straight (rather than curving it out) and feet firmly planted on the floor, push your bottom out as though you're about to sit down. Go out as far as you can.

3. Hold for a count of three.
4. Now push your bottom forwards and tilt it upwards in a kind of scoop as you come up.
5. Repeat from the beginning but this time with your arms stretched straight out from your shoulders in front of you as you go down. Pull them back as though you're rowing as you stand up.
6. Repeat fourteen more times.

OTHER STRETCHING EXERCISES THAT YOU CAN DO:
Yoga, dance movement and martial arts like judo, karate, kung fu, ju jitsu, aikido and kendo.

STRENGTHENING EXERCISES

Don't let anyone ever call you weedy! If you feel fragile, start a course of these to build strength and give you some extra muscle power (though they won't make you muscly): martial arts, weight lifting and resistance exercises such as push ups, sit ups, leg lifts and head lifts (lying on your stomach).

STAMINA AND INTERNAL HEALTH

These are the so-called aerobic exercises because they make you breathe more deeply and strengthen your heart and lungs. This also means you'll be able to run faster and further, if you ever need to! They are: brisk walking, jogging, cycling, swimming (laps) and skipping (with a rope). Also anything that requires repeated movements like step classes.

ALL OVER ACTION

These include the benefits of all of the above and they're probably the most fun to do. They're the sporty ones like squash, tennis, badminton, football, skiing (snow and water), hockey, lacrosse, hurdles, basketball, volleyball, cricket, rounders, bowls, croquet, fast dancing and tossing the javelin or caber!

Wizardry AND YOUR wardrobe

Now let's see how we can decorate this figure that's getting fitter. As I hinted before, it is possible to disguise any bits of your body that you don't like with clothes.

Useful things clothes!

Apart from maintaining your modesty (okay, not shocking other people), clothes can be used to show individuality, style and mood. And besides all that, they keep you warm and are fun to ring the changes in your appearance!

CHARMED CHOICES

Take a look at yourself in the altogether again. (Is this becoming a habit?) What would you rather change?

Is it:

short legs; big thighs; lack of a waist; long arms; short arms; fat shoulders; no neck; no curves; a straight up and down figure; a too round figure; big boobs; small boobs? (I don't know you so I'm not being personal here!)

Write down the important ones. Now look at your clothes. Here are the guidelines:

To make you look slimmer

COLOURS AND PATTERNS:

Dark and dull (black, grey, brown, forest green, navy etc) shades and larger irregular patterns (big dots or daisies) play down larger areas and make you look slimmer. So if your legs are big or short in proportion to the rest of you or you've got chubby thighs, aim for these shades to cover those areas. Don't forget to take your bottom into consideration, too. Large rear ends definitely look at least a size smaller in dark, rather than light, shades. Thin stripes or thin patterns that run downwards will slim you down more than wider ones.

One continuous line, rather than separates (as in a more fitted, rather than loose dress) in a plain dark colour makes you look slimmest of all.

MATERIALS:

Thick fabrics like wool-types or cable sweaters and sweatshirt-type cottons can cover up the odd slight bulge you don't want seen. But they won't disguise a very large figure. Unfortunately, very little can – work on getting slimmer instead.

SHAPES:

You may think that baggy dresses, tops and shorts can hide a lot, but they make shorter, big boned people look fatter (almost round!). You need slim legs and height to get them to disguise a thick waist or big hips. Better for shorter large girls is a slightly fitted (rather than skin tight) dress or, if you've got an okay waist, separates. By the way, a thick belt can help to create a waist, but not if you've too much tummy or too many rolls on the ribs.

To make you look curvier

COLOURS AND PATTERNS:

Bright and light colours (metallics, hot pink, lime green, white, pale blues, yellow etc), bold patterns (big flowers, writing or faces designs) and horizontal (that's sideways) stripes show up that area more. So if you want to look larger or are proud of, say, slim legs, leggings in these kind of shades and patterns are just the thing.

Thin stripes or patterns that run across will show up your curves more. The larger the stripe or directional pattern, the more it shows up your figure.

MATERIALS:

Fine materials like floaty polyesters, silky-type and translucent voiles show up parts you're proud of, like nice shoulders and arms, or a thin waist. They'll also show up parts you're not proud of. Avoid them there.

SHAPES:

Tight fitting clothes show up your curves, though a cleverly cut lycra outfit can hold you in, too. Separates which cut a line at the waist are fine for long waisted people as they show off any curves more.

ARMS TOO LONG

Disguise long arms with three quarter sleeves or long ones pushed up to that length (just below the elbow).

ARMS TOO SHORT

Disguise short arms with cutaway sleeveless tops or sleeves that end just above the elbow.

SHORT NECK

First look at your posture, as described earlier in the chapter, to help keep your shoulders down and make your neck look longer. A polo neck can disguise it. A turtle neck (not rolled over and not quite as high) is even better. A low 'V' neckline also makes your neck look longer.

FAT SHOULDERS

Wear looser sleeves. In the summer stick to short sleeves rather than sleeveless tops.

A Breast of Times

Now a word about boobs. Boobs come in all shapes and sizes. Yours haven't stopped at what they are now. Being flat-chested is very fashionable. Just look at the top models. So don't worry if you haven't much around the chest region.

TO MAKE THEM LOOK BIGGER:

A tight fitting or horizontal stripy top will make more of what you've got. Wearing dresses with darts taking the material in just under the bustline makes them look bigger, too. Making your waist look as small as possible with wide stretchy belts can also make more of what you *don't* have on top.

TO MAKE THEM LOOK SMALLER:

If your boobs have grown at what seems like an alarming rate, remember that you're not used to them being around. What feels to you like two melons on your chest can seem perfectly normal and not very large to other people. You can disguise them with dark or looser fitting tops, if you'd rather.

CUT THE CLOTHES COST

Here are some tips to make you look great on the cheap:

1 Learn how to alter clothes. Change your old clothes to update them or go to shops like Oxfam and find old clothes that you can alter. Shorten skirts and dresses, or add a wide band of contrasting material to the waist and hem to lengthen them. Take off sleeves that look dated to make sleeveless tops and dresses. Take in trousers and jeans for slimmer line legs or make them hipster by lowering the waistband. Cut the legs off old jeans and trousers to make them into shorts for the summer.

2 Customise your clothes for a different look or to cover frayed or stained areas. Add beads or buttons to a plain sweater, braiding round the cuffs and collar of a white or black shirt, patches to the elbows and collar of an old jacket etc.

3 Learn how to make clothes from scratch from patterns and material – it's cheaper and individual.

4 Find lots of interesting materials to make patchwork skirts or waistcoats.

5 Wear things in different ways. Experiment with layering a full old skirt under a shorter new one, an old sweater or shirt under a sleeveless dress, a top back to front for a different look, etc.

SHOP *but* don't drop

Now everyone, and I mean everyone, has bought something they'd rather not be seen dead in. It looked great on someone else. Or was just right in the shop lighting and atmosphere when they tried it on. The trouble is when this wonderful piece of fashion reaches home, the full horror of what they've bought hits them. It doesn't suit them at all. Or some simply mean to wear it sometime but just can't quite find the right occasion.

Sometimes (and this is the worst of all) people wear their fashion mistakes! You see these poor fashion victims – grandmas in silver Lurex, brothers in gangster-style suits, dads in multi-coloured waistcoats or braces, round people in baggy knee length shorts, long people dressed head to foot in huge black and white stripes. Feel sorry for them and make sure it doesn't happen to you!

Think it can't happen to you? It can! But there are some tips to try to prevent it while you're **shopping:**

Take an honest friend with you

Tell her to forget about being polite. You want the truth and nothing but the truth. By the way, make sure the friend has the same taste as you, or is at least looking at things that will suit you rather than her! Actually, if you can ever persuade them, some older brothers are quite good at this kind of advice.

Take the things you want to wear with it

Shoes, top (or bottom) and jewellery etc so you can see how they look together.

Don't impulse buy

Have a pretty clear idea of what you want and where you want to wear it before you go shopping. If you see something else you like, take time to think about it. Go for a cola and think about how it would fit into your wardrobe, where you'd wear it and with what. Also remember your disguise tactics. Is it going to show up things you don't want to reveal too much?

Always try things on

Unless you're sure they'll give you a full cash refund if you return it.

Don't be intimidated by pushy salespeople

They don't know your personality, what you're trying to show up or hide and where you want to wear it. Some (and I'm sure it's only the very worst ones) will say you look great just to get a sale. Simply say, 'I need a few moments to think about it please'. Then go with your own (and your friend's) opinion.

See how it looks on you in realistic surroundings

Shops can be a bit sneaky and tilt their mirrors upwards so you look taller and slimmer. Or they go for soft lighting so you don't notice any bulges or whether it's see-through. After all, they're in the business of selling you the clothes. So if you think you look extra good today, you might! But you also might have just got a flattering mirror! Many a shopper has been caught by great looking mirrors! Make sure you see yourself in a full length, straight on mirror and if possible in daylight. Go and look in another mirror if you suspect the ones near, or in the fitting rooms, are too flattering. But take into account that summer clothes, like a bikini or strappy dress, bought in the spring won't look so good on pasty skin as a tanned body.

Don't forget the angles

Look at yourself in clothes you're trying on side and – this is important – back view, too. After all, people don't see you just from the front!

Try to look at the colour in daylight

Yellow or soft indoor lights can make blue look turquoise, bright subtle and subtle dark. Ask to take it to the window

but make sure an assistant goes with you.

You don't want the tag setting off any alarms!

IF YOU'RE NOT SURE, DON'T DO IT

Ask the shop if they'll keep it for you to come back later or tomorrow. Say you're not sure about it and want to see if it'll go with a top, jewellery etc. Many will do this as long as you give them a decision time. Do be just as nice and go back later, or ring, and say if you DON'T want it.

DON'T...... Grounding

The right shoes can make or break an outfit:

★ If you're on the cuddly side and wearing short skirts higher heels will not make your legs look longer and slimmer. Instead go for a slight heel.

★ Higher heels are fine for slightly skinny legs and normal legs but can make very skinny legs look stick-like. Choose flatties instead.

★ Very high heels and badly fitting shoes will always look strange because you'll be hobbling all the time. They can also damage your feet and back (see the last chapter about buying shoes).

★ Flat shoes, especially with extra thick soles, are flattering to larger legs.

★ Long dark boots and black tights are fantastically flattering – they make everyone's legs look slimmer.

all that glisters...

Apart from being great to wear, jewellery can distract from any parts you want to hide.

For instance:

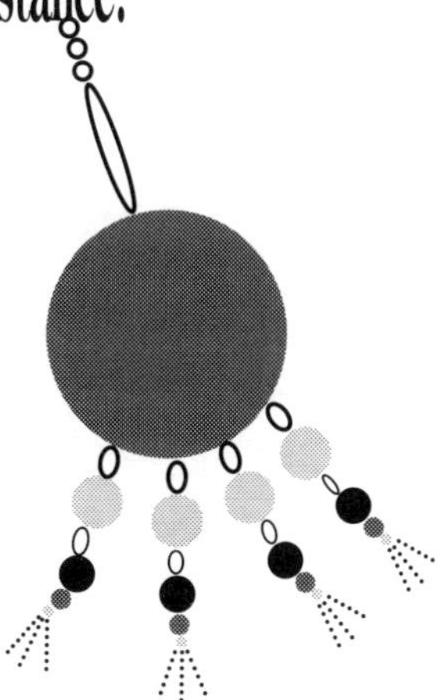

Neck length:

A long necklace ending a few inches above your waist, can act as a V neck and make your neck look longer on a plain colour. A choker will do the opposite. Long dangly ear-rings really only look good on long or normal necks.

A big bust:

A riot of big necklaces around your neckline and chest can detract from a big bust.

Face shape:

Bright, rounder ear-rings look great on thin faces to widen them, but make them extra large and ear length, rather than dangly, on rounder faces.

Short arms:

A big bright bangle or bangles can make short arms look longer.

Skinny arms:

Slim arm (above elbow) bangles can make too thin arms look larger.

Your TRUE colours

By choosing clothes colours to suit your skin and hair colouring you can make yourself look even better and brighter.

Here's a guide to choosing the right kind of colours to suit you. It doesn't take into account that the latest fashion may be black or brown and everyone wants to wear it. So if you want to wear a certain shade and be trendy, go ahead and enjoy it. But if you feel a colour is making you look washed out or flushed these suggestions will help you choose a better colour to flatter your skin tone.

Time to take a look at yourself again!

Choose the best possible light, daylight, to work out your skin colour. We know it's basically white or black. But is your skin more pink, yellow or blue toned?

white skins

If you tan easily and have darker eyebrows and lashes, chances are you have more yellow toned skin. If you burn easily and have pale or red lashes and eyebrows it's more likely to be pinky/red toned. And if you never tan, have dark or white lashes, and your skin has a translucent quality, sometimes showing dark shadows under your eyes or veins, you have blue toned skin.

Black and darker skin

Rosy black skins are pink toned and blue toned black skins are inclined to dark shadows. Lighter black skins and Mediterranean type skins are often yellow toned.

If you're really stuck ask for someone else's opinion or try putting a piece of white card beside your face to give a stark contrast to make it clearer.

Yellow toned skin

This looks great in bright clear colours like deep red, fluorescent pink, clear blue, violet, maroon, white, turquoise, silver etc. But you should avoid oranges, bright yellows, mustard, brown and pillarbox red which echo the yellow in your skin too much and can make you look jaundiced.

Pink toned skin

This looks fabulous in muddy shades and muted colours like strawberry, primrose yellow, grey, cream, terracotta, black, gold etc. Avoid pale pinks, deep red, wine and bronze shades as they can reflect the pinky shades and make you look too flushed.

Blue toned skin

This can look fabulous in soft and earth colours like baby pink, ivory, primrose, sky blue, leaf green, browns, tans and bronze etc. Steer clear of deep or bright shades with blue in them, like blood red, silver grey, navy, mauve, aquamarine etc as they'll reflect on your skin and emphasise the naturally blue shade.

COLOUR

Did you know that the colours you wear can cheer you up or calm you down? The shade of paint in your bedroom or living room can do the same but you can't carry them around with you as therapy!

What you're wearing colour-wise may have already affected your mood. Next time you're in a particularly extreme mood (happy, angry, etc) notice what colour you're wearing. However, you'd be hard pushed to blame colour for bad moods because every colour has a good or bad extreme depending on how you're feeling.

IT'S BETTER JUST TO GO AND CHANGE YOUR CLOTHES!

Here's how to apply some colour therapy:

RED

This is a fiery shade that can get you going if you're feeling weary or fed up. It gives more vitality and energy. It also signals excitement and danger so attracts a lot of attention (that's why we notice fire engines and stop signs), so you have to be sure you want it! Also, if you're feeling tense it can make you more irritable and restless.

Don't wear red to bed – you'll find it harder to get to sleep!

BLUE

This is a calming cool colour, like a clear sky or calm sea. If you feel like you need some soothing or are feeling upset, try putting on a blue sweater. Try also wearing blue on a hot day – it'll make you feel cooler. If you're already feeling tired, blue can send you to sleep, even if you don't want it to, so it's a good one to wear to bed, but it isn't the best shade to wear in company if you want to be lively!

YELLOW

This gives inspiration and **intelligence**. Try to wear something yellow for exams. Yellow is also helpful when you want to be alone to make the right decision about something. The bad side is that it can make you appear a bit detached so it's not the best shade to wear for parties or with friends!

ORANGE

This cheers you up. It's for joy and pleasure. So do wear orange to parties! It encourages movement and dancing. Try an orange dress when you're feeling unsociable but need to join in the fun! It isn't good for studying in libraries or doing your homework, though!

GREEN

This is another relaxing one **(isn't it good that the trees and grass are green?)**. It gives a feeling of harmony and friendship, so wear it when you're trying to help someone at a bad time or need to feel friendlier. It also helps you to feel free if you've been shut in a classroom all day. Too much green can cause indecision and weariness.

TURQUOISE

This is a mix of blue with a touch of yellow (i.e. green) so is soothing, refreshing and helps you work out any problems.

VIOLET

This is a mixture of blue and red so gives feelings of self worth and purpose without the aggravation of pure red.

TRUE BLACK AND VERY DARK BROWN

These are colours which give security. They also create more of whatever emotion you're feeling. So wear them when you want to feel happier and avoid them when you're feeling fed up!

WHITE AND VERY LIGHT CREAM

These make us feel pure and good. Wear them when you've upset someone and you're asking for forgiveness.

If that fails try a soft green, a present and eating very humble pie!

Depth and mixtures of colour can give different effects. For instance, deep blue will have more impact than pale blue. Deep blue can send you to sleep, pale blue can simply relax you. Bright red may irritate you and others but raspberry or mauve (red and blue) can keep you alert. So you can mix your own therapy to help your spirits.

Happy stirring!

Q: Why, oh why, don't the same clothes look as good on me as my friends? And I mean all my friends.

A: Why do you want to look the same as your friends? Have you got the same mothers and fathers? The same personality? The same life? Sounds like you're a bit fed up with yourself. But everyone has something different to offer. The chances are some of your friends are a bit envious of your different style, though they probably wouldn't admit it! Do a bit of research (the above can help) and develop it. Find a type of trademark. Perhaps you could start making your own bracelets and belts with things you can find like rope, shells and stones. Then get really stylish and only wear them on plain grey, black or white clothes. This may not suit you but you get the idea. It may be rolling your sleeves up in a particular way or adding bands of coloured ribbon to the hem of a skirt. Start a trend rather than copying others. Bet you whatever you do they won't look as good, once they've started copying you!

Q: There's no doubt about it. I'm naturally fat. I've found some weight charts and I'm at least two stone overweight. I think I look disgusting but all my family are overweight.

A: Take the matter into your own hands. You alone are responsible for your weight. And while it's much healthier to be a bit over, rather than under, weight; over two stone is unhealthy. Start the process now. Start by expressing your worries to your mum. Tell her you'd like to loose some weight because you'd feel better. If she doesn't agree with you, ask her to go to the doctor with you. The doctor can decide what should be a normal weight for you and how much you need to lose. But if the doctor feels your weight is okay, you should not try to lose any – it could do some damage while you're still growing.

The doctor will probably be able to give you a healthier eating plan. And your mum can help you to slim by not tempting you with too many of the more fattening foods (ask her to hide the biscuits or sweets to put them out of reach). The secret of successful dieting is to eat the same amount so you don't feel hungry just change to healthier, less fattening foods. Cut out all sweets and chocolates – you can keep them as the odd treat. Replace them with fresh fruit and vegetables (it's as easy to buy an apple or orange as a chocolate bar or biscuit). Make your diet as varied as possible and don't cut down on milk and dairy products as calcium is very important while you're still growing.

Far more important and for a great figure, long term, is to start being more active. Start playing tennis, walking the dog (borrow one from someone you know!), swimming, dancing, playing hockey. You'll be surprised how this can lessen your appetite as your body concentrates on sending signals to your muscles instead of your stomach and it distracts you from food. It also makes you feel more energetic and burns up calories, even after you stop. Good luck!

Q: I want my ears pierced so I can wear ear-rings. How do I do it?

A: Not yourself, *please*! People have very different ideas on what age ears should be pierced. In some countries it's traditional to pierce a baby's ears. In Britain it's usually considered a more adult thing to do. So first ask your parents. If they say no, ask when they think you'll be old enough and look forward to that. After all you can still wear clip-on ear-rings, can't you?

If your parents agree, go to a large department store, rather than a little place where you're not so sure of hygiene standards. You should be asked the points where you want the studs first. Then your ears will be cleaned, numbed with some alcohol solution and pierced with a gadget that acts a bit like a stapler. It can hurt! Girls have been known to faint, so it's wise to have someone with you.

You should also be given advice on cleaning and turning the sleeper (the ear-ring they put in to keep the hole open). If you find your ears become infected, treat them with antiseptic. If they're still looking infected after a couple of days, go and see your doctor for treatment.

Q: I've got a collection of tatty old bags, but I'd like a real handbag. Is there any advice on choosing one?

A: There is, but first you have to decide what you want it for: a special occasion, not to carry much; a shoulder bag you can take anywhere; to go with a particular outfit; to replace those tatty ones?

I suspect it's the last one, so here are some ideas. Black and brown colours are the most useful as they go with almost everything and don't show the dirt so much (handbags are dropped on all sorts of floors). Something that hooks over your shoulder is the most useful as it allows you to keep your hands free, so choose either a shoulder strap or backpack type. Plastic and synthetic handbags wear out much quicker than leather, although they're less expensive. Avoid bags with fiddly straps as a) they come off with a lot of wear and b) you're forever doing them up and undoing them. Go for something that can close easily and securely (so you can swing it away from anyone who tries to steal it without losing everything in it!).

Handbags with zippable pockets in them are helpful to put money or tissues in. A last word of advice – don't do like most of us do and put the kitchen sink in your bag. It's very hard on the shoulders!

CHAPTER FOUR

a TOUCH of Colour

Here's what I think about make-up: cleverly applied with a light touch it can make you look great – it can enhance nature and make you feel better. Be your own personal work of art!

Plastering your face with heavy make-up is an entirely different matter. That should only be for:

a kids who want to look like tigers or clowns;
b people in disguise on the run from the police;
c models, film and music stars in specially lit studios to soften the effect;
d shocking other people in the worst possible way!

A riotous mask of colours on the face is not pretty. It is not for:

a girls or women with brains;
b looking attractive or grown up;
c anyone wanting to impress;
d shocking other people in the best possible way!

Did you know the first thing man painted was his/her own body? It's true! But it was less for looking attractive and more to impress – for tribal identity, camouflage while hunting, in magical ceremonies and to frighten off enemies – so it was probably pretty extreme, too.

If you want to start wearing make-up socially or for special occasions it's a good idea to wear a bit in private first so you get used to putting it on properly.

The secret of *good make-up* is to practise with it.
That means putting it on and taking it off quite
a few times until you get the knack.
Beginners with make-up should take
it a step at a time.
You don't need the full works and it will
look funny on a younger face.
Sorry, but there it is!
Start off with a little eye, cheek and lip definition.

Beginner's Beauty

The FIRST rule of beautiful make-up is to see what you're doing!

Find the best lit mirror which is usually one in daylight, rather than electric light, where you can see your face clearly including every eyelash hair. Then work out what you want to achieve. Make-up can make more of your eyes, cheekbones and lips. Or it can be used to disguise (a bad skin, lack of obvious cheekbones) or divert attention from something. For instance if you've a nose you're not proud of, don't wear lipstick. It'll bring the focus to that part of your face. Concentrate on your eyes instead. If you've ears that you hate, keep blusher to a minimum as it draws attention to your temple area, where ears are located.

eyes the windows of your soul

That's what they say eyes are!

Better make them look as lovely as possible then!

Mascara Magic

If you've already got long dark lashes, you don't need mascara. In fact, extra long lashes can look strange and spiky with mascara on them. But if you've got shorter or paler ones, try a non-build up mascara to lengthen your lashes. That's the type without fibres in it to lengthen your lashes. Build up ones can look unnatural on a younger face.

The best mascara shades for pale skins are grey or brown, because they look more natural. Black mascara is suitable for black or dark skinned girls but too heavy for most white skins.

1 Looking into your well lit mirror, put the mascara wand (that's the brush) under your top lashes at their base where your lashes meet your eyelid. You'll have to tilt your head up a bit

(STICKING YOUR TONGUE OUT SOMETIMES HELPS, TOO!).

2 Brush upwards to the ends of the lashes on your top lid.

3 Do the same brushing downwards on the other bottom lashes under your eye.

4 Now, nearly closing one eye, take the mascara wand to the base of the upper lashes and sweep it down to do the top side which shows when your eyes are closed.

5 How does it look? Not enough? Repeat the process.

6 Or is it a bit cloggy? Here's where you need an old cleaned toothbrush. By brushing them after the mascara dries (it only takes a minute to dry) with a toothbrush, a cleaned mascara brush or special mascara comb you can unstick any eyelashes that have stuck together.

Now you're ready for a flutter!

If you've very fair lashes, there's a trick to getting a bit more darkness around your eye: when you begin putting mascara on the top lashes, gently press the brush into your lashline (where it meets the skin). This leaves a bit more mascara at the base of the lashes and rim of your eye and helps to cover fair lashes better.

SHADY SECRETS

You have seen frosted blue or green eyeshadow on some women, haven't you? It's usually not a pretty sight. The only people it really suits are models (or those with model-like faces) who do it as a quirky fashion trend. It makes a statement, but not on girls who want to just make themselves look lovelier. Younger girls shouldn't bother with eyeshadow at all. It won't add anything.

Eyeshadow will look best if you use a natural shade, a bit darker than your skin tone, to add definition to your eyes. By natural I mean those tones that are in your skin: grey/pink, rose, cream, beige, tan or light brown colours. Many come in a combination palate so you can mix them to the shade that suits you best.

Powders are the best to use as they don't smudge or crease so easily and are easier to thin out if you put too much on.

1

Take the applicator or brush and sweep it across the shadow to get some colour on it.

2

Now close one eye and put it to the crease line at the top of your eyelid, where it meets the brow of your eye.
Start the shadow at the point of the crease above your inside eye.

3

Take it along the crease, tapering it up slightly above the outside end of your eye. Stop above the outer corner of your eye.

4

Open your eye and use your judgement. Most people put too much on and this is where cotton wool buds or a creased tissue come in handy. Use one to wipe a bit off.

5

If this doesn't look right, try taking the shadow all over your lid. That's from the crease line down to where your lashes start. But make sure it's a very light cover. You don't want to look too ghoulish and give everyone a fright. Just give your eyes a hint of definition.

WHAT *colour* IS YOUR SKIN?

Time to look at your skin shade again. What's it like? Is it rosy, black, sallow or pale? Now your face shape? Is it more on the round side or thinner?

ROSY SKIN

This has pinky tones and tends to blush easily. Younger rosy skin doesn't need blusher. It'll only make your skin look redder. If you've a round face, however, a tan shade blusher can magic in more cheekbones. Very rosy skin is often called high colour, and given to blushing where you don't want it to! If yours is like this, you might like to try some covering up with a light foundation for special occasions.

BLACK AND SALLOW YELLOW TONED SKIN

Doesn't need covering up as most look healthy and glowing already. If you've got spots, disguise them with concealer or foundation for special occasions. And if yours is pale sallow skin or you've a round face, some blusher can help give you some colour at your cheekbones. If your face is rounder and your skin doesn't need any more glow, choose a tan-type shade to give more definition than radiance.

PALE SKIN

Paler skin can look washed out and you sometimes have dark rings under your eyes. A touch of blusher will brighten it up for special occasions. Go for a pinky or peach shade of blusher to give the appearance of more warmth. But you don't need any covering tactics unless you want to hide problem spotty areas or those dark rings on special occasions.

THINNER FACES

These already have cheekbones on show so they don't need any darker blusher to shape them in. If you've pale or pale sallow skin and a thin face try a warm pinky blusher for a glow on special occasions.

rounder FACES

You can create a hint of cheekbones by shaping them with a deeper tan shade of blusher.

BEST Blushing

Get ready to blush by choosing a shade to suit your skin colour and carefully select the depth of shade. The depth is more to do with how light and dark it is rather than the colour. Match it to the depth of your skin shade. Very pale skins should go for light soft pinks and peaches; sallow skins can take deeper raspberry and brick-type shades (lightly applied, of course).

Powder blushers are easier that cream or solid ones to apply. Simply wipe some off with a tissue if you put too much on.

1

Sweep the brush over the blusher to load it up with colour. Blow off some if you think you've got too much.

2

Use short light strokes on your skin. And remember that if you put too much on you can simply take it off again.

3

For more glow: go for the apples of your cheeks. This is the round fleshy bit. Take the blusher over this part, starting under your mid eye (usually about an inch under it) and stroking the blusher up, outside your eye socket area, tapering it off to your temple.

4

For more defined cheekbones find the point where your cheekbone starts under the middle of your eye. Blush just under and along this line up to your temple.

cover-ups

Soft glowing skin is a beauty asset. Treasure it. Treat it carefully to keep it that way. And be proud of it.

It's pointless to put foundation on good skin – it doesn't need it! Apply eye and cheek colour over it bare. They'll look just as good, if not better!

Not all skin is so perfect, and teenage skin, especially, seems to suffer from spots, rashes and high colour, so you might like to try some cover-ups for special occasions. Foundation should go on first, before eye shadow and blusher if you decide to use it.

Finding a foundation TO SUIT YOU

A tinted moisturiser is a good start to wearing foundation for most girls with fairly good skin. This is basically a moisturiser with some pigment in it to add colour, too. As it's lightly coloured, it allows your natural skin shade to show through while giving a more even skin tone. But it won't cover up large imperfections like acne or rashes.

The miracles of science have now produced foundation formulations which are lighter and yet do more. Now people who wish to cover all sorts of skin problems don't need a thick layer of foundation to do it. Read the packaging to find out which is a good cover but feels light if you'd like to cover skin problems.

IMPORTANT

Now – important this – if you choose a foundation that's vastly different from your own skin shade, it'll look really strange! Your own natural colouring works together. Nature designed it that way. The shades of your eyes, hair, eyebrow colour and skin all compliment each other. Change any one of these dramatically and it looks distinctly freaky. When you're choosing the colour, remember that the back of your hand is a different shade from your face, so it's not worth trying foundation shades there! The best way is to dab a few testers on your jawline. Then rush home to look at them in the mirror in daylight and see which is the nearest to your own skin tone.

If you're finding it difficult to see which foundation is nearest your skin colour, here's a great trick: squint your eyes half closed and see which one disappears first on your skin. That's the one!

Application

1. Apply foundation (and tinted moisturiser, too) to clean skin in small dabs – nose, cheeks, forehead and chin.

2. Now with your fingertips blend them together until the shade is even over your face.

3. Add more if you need to or wipe any excess away with a tissue.

4. **ABRACADABRA!** SMOOTH LOOKING EVEN TONED SKIN!

Getting Lippy

Here's the cruel truth: vivid, dark or bright lipshades look odd on younger faces. So keep the bright reds, vampish maroons and hot pinks for the privacy of your own room. The time will come when they suit your lips. For now, go for the natural lip glossy or pearly shades. They'll look fine and give a hint of poutiness, which is what lipstick is all about. Choose a shade to match your outfit: that's a yellow toned one like transparent peach for yellow based outfits like green, brown or orange or more pale pinky shades for cooler toned outfits like maroon, blue or black. Then just slick it on. The advantage of the lighter glossier ones is that you don't have to be too precise either. Just slide it over your lips like lipsalve.

Making MORE of Make-up

As you get used to make-up you might like to try some of these tips for added effect. They will make you look more made up, so always keep in mind that the warpaint look won't impress in the right way and can scare people off! Take it easy.

DON'T LAY IT ON TOO THICK.

Even though daylight or strong electric light is the best for precision when putting it on, try to look at your make-up in the light you're going to wear it in. Electric, fluorescent or dim night-time light can give different colours and strengths a different effect. A natural looking make-up looks good in most lights.

Pencils are the easiest for creating eye definition. Choose a natural brown, or grey shade. Create a fine line around your eye just outside the base of your lashes with the sharpened point and smudge. Some cosmetic pencils come with smudgers on the other end – very useful!

An ordinary fine painting brush (art painting, not wall!) can help smudge a natural looking line round your eyes.

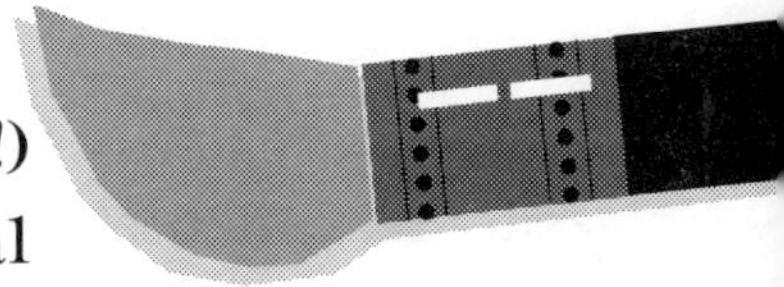

A tawny/tan brown pencil can make a natural looking eyeline and also doubles up as cream blusher if you haven't got any. Lightly pencil it on and smudge it in with your fingertips along your cheekbones.

A bronze powder can be a blusher, eyeshadow or shader (when used more heavily) to create cheekbones. Just because it's called eyeshadow or blusher, it doesn't have to go in those areas.

For a healthier glow, try taking pinky blusher round your temples to the sides of your forehead and dab a touch on your chin.

Tinted moisturisers are the foundation exception when it comes to finding the right colour. As they allow your own skin shade to show through and aren't too heavy, you can go for a tanned one, even on pale skin, in summer. It'll make you look slightly suntanned.

Use petroleum jelly as lipgloss, to make dark eyelashes glisten and look longer and to smooth down wayward eyebrows. It'll also give shine to your lids (just a little). By the way, you can use it as moisturiser on dry skin if you rub a little in well.

Cream eyeshadows and blushers sink into the skin and stay on better, especially in water. Even though you wouldn't want to wear eyeshadow or blusher while swimming, they're best for rainy days when you know you'll be outside. But they melt more easily in heat. Stick to dry powders in sticky situations where you're likely to feel the heat, like at parties or nightclubs.

Some make-up eyeshadows and blushers, that look like powder, are actually creams. Capsules of cream colour are coated in powder to make them go on smoother. Read the labels carefully to see what's what.

The best colours to wear during a busy or frantic day are the natural ones. Flesh tones like pinks and peaches don't show up so much as greys or deep browns when they wear off and get patchy.

Help lipstick or eyeshadow stay in place longer by blotting it with a tissue. Then brush it with face powder and reapply.

Hold stubborn and stuck nail polish tops under hot running water to soften the hardened varnish and help the top come off.

To make the tacky remains of nail polish fluid again, add a few drops of remover to the bottle and shake.

Mix your own shade of polish from two or three others to match your outfit. Simply add drops on some kitchen foil and mix with an old, cleaned nail polish brush. Use quickly before it dries.

Q: I'd like to wear blusher but when I put it on it goes streaky and blobby, even though I'm using powder. Any ideas?

A: The most likely reason is that you have greasy skin or you haven't waited long enough for moisturiser to sink in. These create the same effect. A slippery layer on your skin will make it slip around and streak. Be sure you tone greasier skin well to get rid of any oil. Then use a light moisturiser only if you feel you need one. If your skin is dry or normal and you do need moisturiser, wait at least ten minutes for it to sink in. If it hasn't sunk in by then it could be because you're using one that's too heavy. Try a lighter one or use less to spread it thinner.

You can also get streakiness if you put on too much blusher. Stroke the brush across the blusher and blow off the excess before applying it. Yet another reason could be that your blusher is too dark for you and your natural skin shade is simply showing through. Try a lighter one.

It must be *one* of these! Hope it helps!

Q: Whenever I wear mauve eyeliner or mascara, my eyes itch. Why?

A: Mauve, huh? The answer is that mauve has a red pigment in it which has a higher risk of causing an allergic reaction. And that's what you have. I'll bet it stops when you stop using them. The answer, of course, is to steer clear of these shades completely. Are they really ones you can't live without? Natural colours look much better.

Q: I'd love to wear nail varnish but make a complete mess of it when I put it on. Is there an easy way?

A: Join the club! It's one of the trickiest things to apply and you must make sure it is dry before you touch anything! I firmly believe I have the longest drying nails in history but then I expect everyone does! The art is patience, using thin coats and letting them dry completely before applying another:

1. Shake the bottle thoroughly.
2. Rest your elbow on something solid to give you a steadier hand, or, if you're doing your toenails, separate them with tissues between each toe (but not touching them) so they don't smudge each other.
3. Use a brush loaded with nail polish (but not dripping) and stroke it from base to tip of the nails starting in the middle of each nail and working outwards. Put it on as quickly and evenly as possible to avoid streaks and try to apply as thin a coat as possible.
4. The first coat should be of clear varnish or basecoat. This stops deeper shades seeping into your nails. Deeper colours can leave a yellow tinge to your nails after you've taken it off –

so you look like you smoke a hundred cigarettes a day! Particularly nasty on toenails!

5. Apply a fine coat of colour and let it dry. With very pale pearly shades you may get away with one coat and no base or topcoat. These ones don't show chips or wear so much.

6. If it's darker or a non-pearly matte pale shade you'll probably need a second coat to make it look covered. Apply another thin coat in the same way.

7. Let it dry.

8. To help stop chips and to make it last longer (and we all have better things to do than painting our nails all day!), put on a strengthening topcoat in the same way.

9. Now wait. And wait and wait. The time depends on the thickness of the nail polish and how hot the atmosphere is but usually around an hour.

10. Then when you think it *must* be dry, gently dab a finger on to your largest nail to test it.

11. If it's still tacky, wait another half hour before touching anything. Use a pencil or elbow to open door handles or scratch your nose.

Phew! Is it worth it? Some people think so!

Q: I go red at the slightest thing! And knowing that I'm blushing makes me even more embarrassed. By the way I'm fifteen and have been wearing make-up for a bit. But whatever I wear doesn't cover it.

A: Believe me you are not alone. Lots of well known people have what we call 'high colour' and hate it. There is an answer but it means wearing foundation. Many companies make a green or mauve tinted moisturiser or foundation to wear under a natural colour. This tones down any redness before you put foundation over it. Try it – it works a treat! (Have you noticed any well known people blushing?). By the way, I know this won't help *much* but I'll say it anyway because it's true. Lots of people find blushing charming – especially male people, I'm told!

Q: I've read every book on the subject but my make-up skill is still nil. It always looks a mess. Help!

A: Help is there for the asking. But you may have to put on the entire range of one cosmetic company to get it! Go to a cosmetic company counter in a large department store and ask the consultant if s/he'll give you a free make over. Many companies will do this. Some charge a fee which is redeemable against buying a product. At others you simply make an appointment or they'll do it there and then if they're not busy. These consultants are trained in make-up techniques and can be very helpful. You can pick up some good make-up tricks to suit your face from them.

They do tend only to do it with the more expensive ranges, but you don't have to buy their products, even though their idea is to sell you some (if not the whole range!). It's more honest to go when you are thinking of buying, say, a mascara or blusher, or becoming a customer as you like their colours. But don't be bullied into buying anything. If you're not sure, tell them you'd like to think about it, show a friend or your mum, save up or see your face in daylight before investing in anything. Ask them to put prices to the things you like.

Now some less fortunate news. A few consultants will try to put the whole range on you so you have all the options at once! And many consultants are so involved in their jobs that they tend to layer it on too thick. Cosmetic company chiefs (their bosses) are trying to stamp this out. They're trying to train their consultants to use a lighter touch of make-up. Tell them that you would like an extremely light make-up. Then listen carefully and pick up tips on blusher, eyeshadow and lipstick application.

Another word of warning. Make-up does not need to be put on top of foundation and powder. Many consultants believe that foundation is necessary to keep make-up set and it may help a bit, but it can look much too heavy on young skins – and even older ones sometimes. So take this particular information with a pinch of salt! Adapt their expertise in application and colour, if you like it, to your make-up at home. Good luck!

Q: I have dark circles under my eyes. How can I make them disappear?

A: Are you getting enough sleep? Are you worried about something? Are you eating properly? Have you been ill or suddenly lost weight? All these can cause circles under the eyes and need to be dealt with to make them disappear if you don't normally have them.

Often dark undereye circles are hereditary and run in the family. Unfortunately, apart from the huge step (and not without some risk) of cosmetic surgery laser treatment there isn't much you can do but disguise them.

For lighter shadows use an ordinary foundation. For darker ones try a concealer a slight shade lighter than your skin tone. Check that it isn't too light or you'll end up with white-looking circles under your eyes! A thick pasty lipstick or palate type works better and stays on longer than a liquid one. Use your finger to pat on the foundation or concealer, precisely over the darker areas. Never pull the delicate skin here but lightly stroke it to blend it in where it meets your normal skin colour.
Goodbye shadows!

CHAPTER FIVE

ON THE *Scent*

SMELL IS A FUNNY THING.

In the past, people wore scents to cover up the bad smells – mostly their bad smells. They didn't take baths, you see, so you can imagine how someone smelt after a non-immersed month or so! Or perhaps it's better not to! They used to wear balls of strong smelling flowers or herbs in their clothes. Even earlier this century, most little old ladies smelt of lavender. They had grown up in the days when taking baths was a weekly or monthly, rather than daily affair and the habit of disguising 'natural' stale body smells had stuck. At least I hope that it was a habit rather than still hiding the pong! It put people off wearing lavender scents for quite a while. In fact, poor old lavender has only recently recovered popularity.

These days we wear deodorants which contain scents. They have ingredients to kill the smell-making bacteria in sweat. Anti-perspirants do the same and also restrict the sweat glands and cut down on moisture escaping.

Now that we wash ourselves and our clothes more and most of us wear deodorants, scents are strictly for fun and for making ourselves more attractive people. Although they affect the nose, rather than the eyes as your appearance does, how you smell is very important to other people. Perfume is also a self-indulgent luxury – that's why we give perfumed things as presents so much.

There are smells that some people love, which others hate, like coal or tar. There are smells that remind you of things in your past like baby powder or furniture polish. And then there are smells that people wear; sometimes they can be overpowering. When they're really strong you suspect the person wearing them has a cold and can't smell it themselves, or that they've dropped the perfume bottle over themselves and haven't had time to change. The chances are they just like that smell – strongly like it! It is often hard to smell perfume on yourself, so use it sparingly.

When people smell delicious it draws you to that person so you can smell some more. That's the kind of smell that perfume manufacturers dream of and the kind of balance you should aim to achieve when you use scent.

What is smell?

Smell is as individual as you are. Here's an interesting fact: the tiny particles which create smell, called molecules, go up your nose and send signals to the non-rational side of your brain. They hit you straight on the emotional side, so you recognise and remember a smell before you can describe it. The speech part of your brain is on the rational side and takes longer. Fascinating, huh?

Many fragrance designers use the emotional aspect of smell to create their scents. The designer Jean Paul Gaultier said he wanted to be reminded of his grandmother's baking and nail polish remover when he created his scent. Donna Karan said she wanted her perfume to smell a bit like her husband's neck! Strangely enough both these fragrances are big sellers, so obviously these smells are popular with other people, too!

Fragrance

Perfumes are divided into different families, related by having the same type of ingredients in them.

Here they are:

FLORAL

These are the most popular perfumes of all. They're flowery and pretty. Classic florals are: Anais Anais by Cacharel, Chloe by Lagerfeld, Joy by Jean Patou, L'Air du Temps by Ricci, Interdit by Givenchy, White Linen by Estée Lauder and Paris by Yves Saint Laurent.

FLORIENTAL

As the name suggests these are mixtures of floral and oriental, so they're pretty but with an air of magical spice. Classics are: Lou Lou by Cacharel, Diva by Ungaro, Jean Paul Gaultier and Escada.

GREEN

These give a grassy or leafy impression using herbs, ferns, mosses and sometimes citrus. Classics are: Vent Vert by Balmain and Halston's Catalyst for Men.

ORIENTAL

These perfumes conjure up warm mystical images with spices like nutmeg, cinnamon and vanilla to remind you of the Orient (ask your geography teacher!). Classic orientals are: Opium by Yves St Laurent, Coco by Chanel, Shalimar by Guerlain, Obsession by Calvin Klein, Donna Karan and Youth Dew by Estée Lauder.

CHYPRE

This family of exotic scents is named after the original blend from Cyprus containing oakmoss and patchouli, sometimes with fruity tones and sandalwood. Classics are: Fendi, Miss Balmain, Mitsouko and Givenchy III.

Families

AQUATIC

This family uses natural ingredients like verbena, water lily and nutmeg to create a fresh smell which reminds you of water. Classics are: Armani Acqua di Gio, Eden by Cacharel and L'Eau D'Issey Pour Homme.

CITRUS

The lively, zingy smell from citrus fruits is often used for sporty-type scents. Classics are: Safari by Ralph Lauren, Sunflowers by Elizabeth Arden, O de Lancome and Eau de Guerlain.

ALDEHYDIC

These are made from all synthetic ingredients and include perfumes like K de Krizia and Arpege (which has floral ingredients, too).

OZONIC/OCEANIC

These names are used to describe fresh, outdoor and sea-type smells with synthetic ingredients and a strong lasting first impression (or top note, see below). Classics are: Escape by Calvin Klein and Aramis New West Skinscent for Her.

FOUGÈRE AND LEATHER

These are rarely around now and are mainly 'masculine' smells with lavender, leather, tobacco and moss.

Often a scent is a mixture of two or more families. For instance Y by Yves Saint Laurent is a green/chypre and Wrappings by Clinique is a green/floral.

How to select a Scent

So how do you go about picking a particular perfume? Well, first you could look at the list above and decide what kind of impression you'd like to create: floral and pretty, oriental and magical, citrus and lively etc. After that, there's only one way. The proof of the pudding is in the eating. Or, perhaps we should say, in the smelling.

1 The best place to smell perfume, for testing purposes, is on your inside wrists and inside elbows where it can reach your nose, close up!

Before you go to test any scents, make sure the skin on your lower arms is dry, clean and hasn't any fragrance on it. Wash off any scent from a shower gel/bath oil or a body lotion with unperfumed soap.

2 Go to a large department store where they have many different perfumes for sale, with testers. Testers are just ordinary perfume sprays for anyone who is thinking of buying that particular fragrance to try out.

3 Your nose can't smell more than about four scents properly at the same time. It'll need a rest afterwards for a few hours. So choose four fragrances that you think you might like. Look at the packaging and ask the salespeople for a description. Pick out four which appeal to you.

Each perfume comes with a profile. This profile explains the type of person they were created for: young, sophisticated, independent, carefree, wild, wacky, designer, summery etc. You don't have to choose one that fits you but it might help you choose some to try.

4 Spray them, one on each wrist and each inside of your elbow, smelling each one in turn after spraying. The initial impression you get is called the top note. It's the first 'phase' of the perfume.

5 Most perfumes change after a few minutes, so the top note goes and another similar scent emerges. Smell them again after you've walked around a bit. This next smell is called the heart or middle note of the perfume.

6 It changes again as it fades away, so have another good whiff after a couple of hours or so. This is called the bottom or base note. The bottom note is probably the most important one as it's the one that stays on your skin until it wears or washes off. But perfume is very expensive, you really need to like all three notes, or phases, to be sure before you buy.

7 You may be surprised at how different one perfume can smell, not only on different people, but at different times on you. That's because it mixes with your own natural (washed!) smells which change according to what you've been eating, your state of health, the time of the year, etc. So if a perfume suddenly smells different on you, ask yourself if you've been eating garlic or rushing around recently!

Perfume goes off after a year or two, and even sooner if it's left in daylight or warm places like in front of a window. The best place to preserve it for longer is a cool, dark place. Putting it in the fridge in hot weather will make it last longer.

BODY Building

A way of making perfume last longer on you is to 'layer' it.

Layering means using several products from the same fragrance range at the same time, and it gives you a top to toe smell – for instance, washing with the shower/bath gel or soap, then spraying on the deodorant and patting on the body lotion. Then you can use the scent to spray on your pulse spots.

Your pulse spots are warmer places so the smell radiates faster. They are behind your ears, your wrists, inside your elbows, behind your knees and at the base of your neck.

Some ranges even include bath oils, talcs, body creams for dry skin, spray oils for a skin sheen, body sprays as an all over deodorant, hair shampoos and conditioners.

But remember that although these other products aren't so highly concentrated and so don't smell so much, you can overdo it! If you're lucky enough to have the whole range, you may like to start with the soap or bath oil or shower gel and spray eau de toilette and collect the others for special occasions.

The bath and body products make excellent birthday or Christmas presents from people who don't know what to get you – and vice versa!

Mix & Match

HOW ABOUT MAKING YOUR OWN PERFUME?

It's a great idea if you can't afford the expense of perfumes in the shops. Making your own scent may not be the sophisticated mix you can buy in the shops but it can be your own personal, individual scent. First you need to find the essential ingredients: flowers and/or plants. Then decide if you'd like a light scented water or a moisturising oil to put on.

For your own individual fragrance first find smells that you like from flowers and plants. Flowers like daffodils, primroses, roses, lavender, lily of the valley, violets, fuschias, jasmine, iris, lilies or honeysuckle can all be used. Or seek out plants, fruits or herbs where you like the smell: vanilla, strawberry, peach, orange, avocado, rosemary, nutmeg, bay leaves, cinnamon, ginger, almond or pine, for instance. Try mixing and matching several together until you find a nice fragrant aroma.

Press your collected flowers and/or plants tightly into a small jar with an airtight lid, like a small clean jam jar. Cut them into smaller pieces if necessary. It's important to fill the jar to the top and put the lid on tightly so that the mixture doesn't go 'off' with exposure to air.

For perfumed oil, add the most odourless vegetable oil you can find, like wheatgerm, or find one at a health store, like almond or coconut oil used as carrier oils for aromatherapy (these will have a faint scent of their own). Pour it over the top, making sure that it soaks the plants. Put on the lid tightly. Leave the jar in a warm place for a couple of weeks. Then strain off the scented oil and keep it. Throw the flower/plant mix away.

For perfumed water, add warm water, instead of oil, to soak the ingredients in your tightly packed jar. Make sure the lid is on tight and leave it to 'steep' for a week or so. Strain and discard the flower/plant bulk, keeping the scented water to splash on.

Like all natural products without preservatives, these will go off when exposed to air and daylight for a week or so depending on the heat and light they're in. Keep them in the fridge to help them last longer, if your mum agrees. They're also *more* likely to cause an allergic reaction so steer clear of them if your skin starts tingling. If you have any clear and odourless chemical alcohol (like rubbing alcohol) add a drop or two to the oil or water and shake the jar to help preserve them for longer.

If your individual mix of perfume is a success, dab it on your pulse spots, but let it sink in before you put clothes on or you could mark them.

Questions Answers

Q: *My twin sister and I both like the same scent, but it smells great on her and horrible on me. Why?*

A: It's because you're not the same person. You eat different things, get ill at different times, probably have different chemical make ups unless you're identical. And what you do, as well as how you are, makes a difference with smell. For instance, if identical twins are sprayed with scent, then one runs five miles and the other stands still, it's going to smell different on each of them afterwards. Find a scent that you love and that suits you.

Q: *If I spray anything perfumed on my skin I come up in big red bumps. I'd like to smell gorgeous but how can I?*

A: We usually spray perfume on pulse spots, like inside the wrists, behind the ears and around the neck. But as your skin is allergic to scent, you must avoid spraying on it. Instead try a light (or the oil in the perfume will mark) spray on light coloured (or the alcohol in the perfume will fade the material) cuffs, collars and headbands etc of clothes that can be washed easily, before you put them on. Spray behind the lapels or cuffs if you can. Another idea is to copy the old days and give a handkerchief a good spray before putting it in a pocket. You can dab it on to your hair if it's thick and there's no chance of it getting to your skin.

You may just be allergic to one type of ingredient, most likely a natural one, in fragrances. Allergies can come and go without any obvious reason, so patch test other ones occasionally (just in one area, like inside your elbow, so any reaction, if it happens, won't be so noticeable), or find the synthetic-made ones without any natural ingredients. Synthetic fragrances may sound awful but, like chemically-made skincare, they are more stable to outside influences like light and warmth and so don't disintegrate or cause skin reactions so easily. Alternatively, you may be allergic to alcohol which is in most shop-bought fragrances. Try a fragranced body lotion without alcohol (read the packaging or ask the chemist or consultant). Happy sniffing!

Q: ***What's the difference between perfume, scent and fragrance?***

A: Nothing at all! Perfume originally meant 'through smoke' as substances were burnt to give off a pleasant smell, a bit like incense. Now they all mean the same thing – a liquid in a bottle to make you smell good!

Q: ***What's the difference between cologne, eau de toilette and perfume? And why do some of these last longer on me than others?***

A: It's all to do with the percentage of pure oil essence (that is the smelly plant or synthetic part) compared to the liquid, which is alcohol. Alcohol is used to preserve the fragrance in the bottle and then it evaporates on your skin so the oils don't feel sticky. Perfume is fifteen to thirty per cent pure concentrated oil essence and is meant to last up to six hours. Eau de parfum is eight to fifteen per cent and lasts up to five hours. Eau de toilette is five to ten per cent and lingers for up to four hours. Cologne, or body spray, is the weakest at two to five per cent, lasting up to two hours before it needs respraying.

CHAPTER SIX

THE FORGOTTEN *bits*

Here is a quiz for you:

What are always ready to take you to places you want to go to, quickly avoid places you don't want to be, allow you to see higher than your height and support you for hours on end, mainly without complaining?

Answer: your feet!

Now: what helps you to open doors, write, dress yourself, point, beckon, wave, play the piano if you wish and generally care for yourself?

You've got it - your hands!

And what things do you talk to others and eat with, gather information from the outside world with and rest on when you're weary?

Your mouth, eyes and bottom, that's what!

These bits of the body are useful, aren't they? But how long do you spend caring for your feet, hands, teeth, eyes and behind compared to your clothes, hair and make-up? My guess is not so long. Most of us don't. These forgotten beauty areas of the body work really hard for us. They support us and help us to relax, play or do whatever we want to do. In doing these jobs they get more wear and tear than almost anywhere else, but they're the parts we most neglect. Now's the time to give them a break. Care for your forgotten bits as you do for your skin or hair and you'll find that they serve you better for longer without trouble. They'll also look better and give you an overall picture of glowing good looks and health.

First Feet

Tired, neglected feet soon let you know how they feel! The pain is directly reflected on your face and is not a pretty sight!

In fact, feet that hurt affect your whole body and they also show that you are causing them damage. Most people's feet keep on growing until the age of twenty-one – that's longer than the rest of your body which usually stops at around eighteen. So your feet are still forming and you need to be careful not to do anything that damages them during this vulnerable time. By looking after and caring for your feet you'll be proud to let them be seen. You can paint your toenails an attractive colour in summer and wear sandals to show them off.

The worst thing you can do to your feet is be overweight which puts more strain on them, or wear badly-fitting shoes which can deform them and make your posture bad.

Shoes

Because our feet are vulnerable to cold weather and abrasive surfaces they need protection with shoes. Shoes are also part of your overall look and badly chosen or fitting shoes can ruin the look of an otherwise great outfit.

Here are some tips:

1 As your feet are still growing, get your shoe size checked every time you buy a new pair. By the way, you should always do this as even when they're fully grown, your feet change shape and spread as you get older.

2 If you are short and want some height, or want to make your legs look longer, very high heels are not the answer. They look as though you're obviously trying to look taller and also push your foot forwards and squash your toes. Instead, go for a slight heel or thicker sole with a lower cut front of the shoe to make your legs look longer.

3 Legs which are too thin look best in flat shoes.

4 If you feel your feet are too big wear dark (black or brown) or neutral (beige, tan, cream) shades so as not to bring attention to them.

5 Shoes don't need to match the colour of your clothes but to look good they should blend with them, matching a colour in the pattern or being a lighter or darker shade. For instance, gold shoes look good with cream clothes as they're both yellow-based, grey shoes go with blue as they're both cool tones. Alternatively, choose a shoe colour to match your handbag, some jewellery, even nail polish. Contrasting shoes can make a fashion statement if you feel confident that your feet and legs look good and you don't mind bringing attention to them: bright orange shoes with a hot pink short dress, red shoes with a white skirt/shorts and a stripy blue and white top, for example.

6 The best shoes to make you and your feet look and feel comfortable should fit well and not slip as you walk or squeeze your toes. They should be around half an inch longer than your longest toe – which isn't always the big one – and have plenty of room for your toes to move. They should fit snugly at the heel and also hold the arch of your foot in the shoe so you don't have to grip your toes to keep them on. Boots (which look good on everyone), lace-ups and those with a cross-strap are better for your feet than very low cut 'court' shoes which leave the top of your feet open.

Foot *care*

Give your feet some tender loving care to keep them smooth and glowing with good looks:

1 If your feet have rough dry patches, gently rub them away with a pumice stone or rough flannel in the bath or shower when the skin is softer.

★

2 Dry between your toes carefully to help prevent athlete's foot (an itchy raw fungal condition – get advice from the chemist). Inspect them for verrucae (a kind of foot wart – see your chemist, or doctor for stubborn ones) at this time, too.

★

3 Now's the time to cut your toenails if they need it. Use small nail scissors and cut them straight across. File away any jagged edges making sure you don't file down at the sides.

★

4 Gently push back your cuticles with your thumbnail. The cuticles (it's the same name as those overlapping tiles on your hair) are the skin at the base of your nails which can grow over the half moon shape there. When they do this, the area is more likely to get dry and cause cracking and hangnails (yes, even on feet). It doesn't look very nice either.

★

5 Give your toenails, feet and legs a good moisturising treatment after a bath or shower by stroking on some body or baby lotion. This will seal in the moisture and stop them getting dry.

Special foot lotions or creams from the shops are designed to cool them down and keep them soft and fresh smelling. They're useful when it's hot: foot odour is not attractive. Try foot deodorant/anti-perspirant sprays or powders to help prevent foot odour when your feet get hot and are enclosed in thick tights and shoes or boots all day. Another cooling down trick for feet is to use a plastic plant spray bottle filled with water and give them a quick blast when they get hot, then let them dry off naturally.

After allowing moisturiser to sink in, now is the time to paint your toenails if you wish. Allow your toenails to 'breathe' by not wearing nail polish all the time. A week on and a week off (except during holidays) is a good rule and leave them polish-free in the winter when they don't show. See under the Trouble-shooting section for more information.

Playing Footsy

If your feet are tired or hot and swollen, try lying down with them straight out and higher than your head for at least fifteen minutes.

Quicker exercises to relieve tired feet and keep them supple and healthy are:

1

Sitting down, straighten the knee of one leg and point the toes of that foot. Now make circles in the air, revolving your feet from the ankles. Do it twenty times, first in one direction then the other. Repeat with the other leg.

2

Still sitting, lift your heels and press your toes hard into the floor. Keep them there for a slow count of ten. Then reverse it by pressing your ankles into the floor with your toes off the ground to a count of ten. Repeat this ten times.

3

Now try to pick up a pencil with the toes on one foot, then the other.

4

Find a cold empty bottle or drinks can and roll each foot over it, back and forth twenty times. This is a great pick-me-up for tired feet, too!

HELPING Hands

Your hands are almost always on show, along with your face. But while faces get all the attention, hands do the hard work. Reward them and keep them looking lovely by moisturising them at least twice daily (more if they're dry) with applications of hand or body cream. Wear warm gloves to protect them from cold weather, rubber gloves when they are in detergents doing washing-up or some housework and thick gloves to prevent scrapping and chaffing when you're gardening or doing building or mechanical work.

Do yourself and your hands a favour by giving them a thorough manicure every two weeks. You can do this in a spare half hour while watching television.

manicure

For a manicure you'll need nail polish remover (if you've got varnish on), cotton wool or tissues, a pair of nail scissors, an emery board, some warm water in a big bowl and some handcream or thick body lotion.

1 Remove all nail polish with the remover and cotton wool or tissue. Gently dabbing into the nail, rather than scrubbing at it, works better to dissolve the varnish before wiping it off.

2 Then soak your nails in the bowl of warm water for ten minutes until your nails and the skin around them are soft.

3 If they need to be a lot shorter, cut your fingernails into a gently rounded shape with the scissors. The ideal practical length is the same height or up to one eighth of an inch over your fingertip.

4 While the skin is still soft, gently push back the cuticles, where the skin grows at the base of the nail, with your thumbnail. Make sure that the half moon white area at the base of the nail shows. This will prevent hangnails forming.

5 File your nails with the emery board if they only need a little amount taken off, they need shaping or there are some jagged edges that will snag on things. File in one direction rather than in a scrubbing motion back and forth, as it is gentler and less likely to damage the nails and cause them to split. Shape them to a softened square or rounded shape. Make sure you don't file too far down into the skin at the sides where the nail joins with your skin.

6 Gently scrape the end of the emery board under your nail tips to remove any dirt or nail filings there and give you nice whiter nail tips.

7 Apply a good dollop of handcream or body lotion and massage your hands to help the circulation and to keep your nails healthy.

Start smoothing the handcream all over one hand using the fingers and thumb of the other one. Go down each finger and the thumb and over the palms as if you're putting on a tight glove. Now go the other way, starting at your wrist and gently massaging up your palm with tiny circular motions. Do it two or three times from wrist to finger base, until you've covered the whole palm. Now start on the fingers. Gripping each one in turn, go from the base up to the tip, gently squeezing as you massage. Make sure you massage plenty of cream into your nails and cuticles. When you've done them all, including your thumb, reverse the process. Start at your finger tips and go down your palm, ending at your wrist. Now do the other hand.

Hand movements

EXERCISING YOUR HANDS HELPS TO KEEP THEM SUPPLE, TONED AND HEALTHY. DO THESE EXERCISES ESPECIALLY IN COLD WEATHER OR IF YOUR HANDS GET SWOLLEN IN HOT WEATHER OR ON AEROPLANES:

1 Stretch them by straightening your arms right out from the shoulder and spreading your hands as wide as possible for a few seconds. Then let them go limp. Repeat this ten times.

2 Now circle them at the wrists in one direction, then the other, ten times each.

3 Point each finger (and thumb) in turn for a few seconds.

4 Pretend to play the piano or type for a minute or two.

Handy

PERSONALITY

hints...

According to ancient philosophy your hands show a lot about your character:

BIG HANDS
mean that you're capable and calm.

SMALL HANDS
show that you're more likely to take risks and react quickly.

ANGULAR HANDS
indicate practicality and a sensible person.

ROUNDER HANDS
show sensitivity and an emotional person.

BROAD FINGERS
show an open-minded attitude, tolerance and generosity.

SQUARE-SHAPED FINGERS
mean that you're rational and disciplined.

LONG FINGERS
mean you're proud, artistic and temperamental.

SHORT FINGERS
show a practical, stubborn and determined streak.

A Winning Smile

As I mentioned right at the beginning, a bright smile makes you nicer to know. But make sure yours *is* bright and not dingy due to bad toothcare. Stained, unhealthy-looking teeth are as much of a turn-off as greasy unwashed hair or body odour. So remember to look after your teeth with regular dental check-ups (every six months), by brushing at least twice a day and by flossing once a day after brushing.

Stained *teeth*

SOME TEETH ARE NATURALLY MORE WHITE THAN OTHERS. JUST LIKE SKIN OR EYE COLOUR, WE HAVE DIFFERENT SHADES, BUT STAINED TEETH CAN BE CAUSED BY PLAQUE FROM NOT CLEANING THEM PROPERLY OR TOBACCO, RED WINE, COFFEE AND SOME FOOD DYES. LUCKILY THEY CAN BE BROUGHT BACK TO THEIR BEST BRIGHTNESS WITH HYGIENIST TREATMENT AT THE DENTIST AND REGULAR BRUSHING AFTERWARDS. BUT IF YOU LEAVE PLAQUE ON YOUR TEETH FOR TOO LONG IT CAN DO DAMAGE TO THE ENAMEL, EVENTUALLY CAUSING HOLES THAT NEED FILLING. EVEN WORSE, IT CAN CAUSE DAMAGE UNDER THE GUM AND GUM DISEASE THAT RUNS THE RISK OF YOU LOSING YOUR TEETH IF IT'S ALLOWED TO SPREAD!

About plaque

Plaque is a bi-product of the bacteria in your mouth and food. It's a nearly invisible (except when stained) jelly-like substance which is good at sticking to the teeth. If left on the teeth it breaks down further and starts to inflame the gums and become acidic, causing tooth decay. Tartar is hardened plaque which allows more plaque to cling more easily.

How to brush

To protect your precious teeth from the harmful influence of plaque and tartar, brush them first thing in the morning and last thing at night.

Brushing your teeth thoroughly should take about two minutes. Time it if you're not sure.

Make sure your toothbrush is in a good state. They should be changed at least every two months. Small headed brushes are most effective as they'll reach more areas. Use a fluoride toothpaste or one with baking soda in it if you have discoloured teeth and want to make them brighter. Don't brush too hard or you can damage your gums. Brush in small gentle circles over each side and the top of each tooth. After rinsing, floss them by using dental floss or tape between each tooth to remove any stubborn particles trapped there.

Avoid brushing your teeth just after eating anything acidic (i.e. citrus fruits or juices) or sweet as these soften the enamel that covers your teeth and brushing can damage it. Wait for half an hour. If you really need to freshen your mouth immediately, it's better to use a mouthwash or chew sugarless gum to remove particles and create saliva which helps to protect teeth.

About Dentists

I don't know anyone who likes going to the dentist, although most dentists are perfectly nice people. They certainly have the best for your teeth in mind. It's their job.

If you're terrified, let the dentist know. They have all been trained in helping people who fear going to the dentist – some are probably a bit afraid of going to have their teeth checked themselves! And they'd rather be warned than have you going into a dead faint or suddenly jumping out of the chair.

Your dentist should tell you what's likely to hurt, if you ask him or her. If s/he doesn't or you feel that they're suggesting too much or too little work on your teeth, talk it over with your mum or dad. You can go and get a second opinion from another dentist. If you don't like your dentist, think the surgery isn't as clean as it could be, or hear that another one has better facilities (like a separate hygienist or more modern equipment) you can also change. Friends and neighbours are the best people to recommend a good local dentist.

Bad Breath

This can be caused by bad teeth and gums, or it can be because of stomach complaints, hormonal imbalances (many women suffer from bad breath pre-menstrually), eating spicy foods or smoking. Try chewing parsley or mint to ease bad breath. Otherwise opt for one of the mouthwashes available at the chemist. If all else fails, see your doctor.

Special Dental Techniques

There's no reason to suffer with crooked, very gappy or ugly teeth these days. Dental techniques have made great strides and some cosmetic dentistry is paid for by the NHS. Ask what can be done to make your teeth look as good as possible. Don't forget to ask for the whole cost, including returning for check-ups afterwards.

BRIGHT eyes

YOUR EYES SERVE YOU EVERY MINUTE OF THE WAKING DAY.

The lens muscles in your eyes work harder than any others, moving around 100,000 times a day and blinking around six million times a year! Your eyes are also one of your best beauty assets. They reflect any emotions you are feeling, your health and your character. Having the best possible sight is vital for avoiding danger and appreciating the world. Have your eyes tested by an optician every year. Talk to your optician and see below, in the Trouble-shooting section, for further advice if you need glasses.

SUNGLASSES

Sunglasses can protect your eyes from the harmful rays of the sun, especially when you're sunbathing – and they can look good too. See under the Trouble-shooting section for advice on finding frames to suit you. Never look directly into the sun even on cloudy days. Wearing sunglasses when driving (a bicycle, a horse) or needing to see clearly outside cuts down glare and helps prevent accidents. Look out for the British Approved Standard ones with the code BS 2724:1987 on them. Badly made dark lenses can distort your vision and cause headaches and eye problems.

FOR CLEARER, BRIGHTER EYES

The best eye-wash is tears and the best beauty treatment, sleep. If you can't achieve these, try soaking two ordinary tea bags under the cold tap and then put them in the fridge for an hour. Lie down and place one over each eye for at least fifteen minutes. Thin slices of cold raw potato on normal skin and cucumber on greasier skin will freshen them up if used in the same way.

On the odd occasions when eyes are especially tired or irritated and you need them to look brighter try eyewashes from the chemist or one made from the herb eyebright, from a health store. It's important that anything you put in your eye is safe and not contaminated by bacteria so make sure you wash your hands, containers and eyebath thoroughly before starting. Mix a teaspoon of eyebright (also called euphrasia) with three fluid ounces of boiling water in a clean container. Cover and allow it to cool down completely. Strain carefully so there are no bits in it. Use the liquid to bathe your eyes in an eyebath or add drops to your eye with a clean tissue – not cotton wool as the fibres can get into your eyes and irritate them more. Remake the eyewash each time you need it to avoid infection. Alternatively, add two drops of tincture of eyebright to a clean eyebath full of boiled and cooled water.

To *revitalise* TIRED EYES

TRY SOME RELAXATION TECHNIQUES IN A QUIET MOMENT. SIT COMFORTABLY, WITH YOUR SHOULDERS DOWN AND YOUR HEAD UP.

1

Keeping your head still, look as far to the left as you can, then as far to the right as you can. Look up to between your eyebrows and down to the tip of your nose. Then circle your eyes three times, trying to see around your eyelashes.

2

Now squeeze your eyes tight shut for a second and then open them as wide as you can. Repeat this three times.

3

CLOSE YOUR EYES, PLACE YOUR PALMS AND FINGERS UP ON YOUR FOREHEAD, OVER YOUR EYES AND BREATHE IN AND OUT SLOWLY THREE TIMES.

Tired eyes from using computer screens

Most schools have had expert advice on where to put computers in the best possible light for you to work on them. Make sure you do the same if you have one at home. There should be adequate light to see the screen properly but no glare from a window right behind it or you. Adjust your seating level on a fixed screen or tilt a levered screen to make sure you have the best angle to see the screen type. Take regular breaks from looking at the screen. Every fifteen minutes make sure you look away and focus on things in the distance for a minute or so. Remember to blink to keep your eyes moist. Use an eyewash, as above, if they feel dry and itchy.

eye PROBLEMS

Unlike your skin or hair, your eyes can't renew themselves. Take eye problems very seriously. Make sure you deal with eye soreness, pain or irritation quickly. If you can't remedy problems quickly yourself or the pain is sudden, see a doctor or go to an accident department in a hospital immediately.

Crying is good for the eyes!
And although animals' eyes water, a good sob is unique to humans! It lubricates and cleans the eyes and scientists say it helps to relieve stress. So, if you feel like it, give in to a good cry.
But don't rub your eyes as this can cause damage.

Bits in your eye (like dust, grit, eyelashes etc) called 'foreign bodies':
If gentle dabbing with a tissue doesn't work, try rinsing out your eyes with clear water or an eyewash.
See a doctor if it's painful or this doesn't work.

DRY EYES:
Treat as above, but if they get painful it could be caused by a blocked tear duct, in which case see a doctor.

Itchy eyes:
These could be because they're dry and irritated from arid or dusty atmospheres or simply tired. Eye drops and a good amount of shut eye should cure it. Red and itchy eyes could be an allergy or viral infection called conjunctivitis.
See your doctor.

FLAKY EYELIDS (BLEPHARITIS):
Sore and dry irritation at the edge of the eyelid is caused by allergy or a kind of eyelash dandruff. See your doctor.

STYE:
This is an infection in one of the sebaceous glands around the eyelash – a bit like a boil. The eye should be bathed three times a day in warm water with a pinch of salt dissolved in it. If it doesn't go down after twenty-four hours or it recurs often see your doctor.

DARK UNDEREYE SHADOWS:
This can be hereditary or caused by lack of sleep or illness. See Chapter 4 on how to conceal them.

PUFFY EYES:
These are usually from lack of sleep or crying. Bathe them in cold water or an eyewash. Occasionally puffy eyes are caused by allergy – see your doctor.

EYESIGHT:
The most common problems which require glasses (see the Trouble-shooting section for advice on frames) or contact lenses are:

Short sight (myopia):
where objects in the distance are out of focus.

Long sight (hypermetropia):
where you can't see objects close up. This is the one which most affects people as they get older.

Astigmatism:
is a structure defect in the eye which causes blurred vision. Sometimes contact lenses are not suitable because of the shape of the eye.

Cross eyes:
need to be corrected by special glasses and sometimes an operation to prevent one eye becoming much weaker than the other.

CONTACT LENSES

Hard lenses just cover the black pupil area. They are now almost all gas permeable which allows the eye to 'breathe' and makes them more comfortable to wear. Soft lenses cover the whole iris (coloured part of the eye) and contain a higher water content to make them more flexible and easier to wear. They don't last as long as hard lenses. You can get soft lenses which are coloured to change or brighten your eye colour or disposable ones which you simply throw away after wearing.

BACK TO THE *Future*

Most animals don't have a fleshy round cushion on their hind quarters because they don't need one to rest on when they sit down. But the human backside provides a comfortable seat to sit on. It's also a reserve fat supply which nature supplies to women for when they get pregnant to make sure the baby gets enough nutrition.

Your rear end is the most difficult part of yourself to see, and unfortunately, one of the easiest for others to view! Take some time to make it firmer and trimmer:

EXERCISES

THE BEST WAY TO FIRM UP A WOBBLY BOTTOM IS, LIKE THE REST OF YOUR BODY, THROUGH EXERCISE.

TRY THESE THREE TIMES A WEEK:

1 Stand straight and without bending your back, stick one leg out straight behind you with the toe pointed. Take it up as far behind you as you can, keeping the leg straight.

Repeat ten times and then with the other leg.

• • •

2 Still standing straight, kick one leg out to the side as far as you can, keeping your toes up (not pointed). Hold it there for a count of ten and repeat three times.

Repeat with the other leg.

• • •

3 Place your feet about two metres apart, turning your toes out slightly but keeping your feet flat on the ground. Make sure that your knees are out and, keeping them directly above your ankles, slowly go down. Keep your back straight and your bottom in all the time. Hold for a count of three and slowly come up.

Repeat ten times.

• • •

4 Any time, any place, sitting or standing, clench your buttocks together as hard as you can. Hold for a count of three and release.

Repeat ten times.

Fatty bum bum...

Pinching, banging or slapping any wobbly bits won't help firm them and may do damage or bruise you. For instance, going down the stairs on just your bottom can jar and bruise your spine. 'Walking' across a softer (carpeted) floor on your bottom may help a bit if you do it in moderation (gently and no more than a minute a day), but it's not as good as the exercises above and you should stop if it feels painful. Better by far are the exercises above to tone up the underlying muscles, combined with gentle massage to tone up the top skin.

Try massaging fattier areas in the bath or shower. This gets the circulation going underneath your skin and helps to dispel any waterlogged fat there. You should feel it but it should not hurt. Use some soapy lather and gently knead the wobbly parts you want to disappear with your knuckles in circular motions. Aim not to pull or stretch the skin as this can make it worse. Try instead to press firmly on to the skin.

DIMPLY SKIN

If you have goosebump-type skin or spotty areas use a rough flannel over your knuckles or a loofah to knead the skin on your bottom. Be gentle – you don't want grazes. Treat spotty skin as you would anywhere else, using a drying out lotion like antiseptic liquid or a spot treatment cream like benzoyl peroxide on larger spots. When it's possible, avoid wearing tight-fitting and synthetic clothes like tight jeans or lycra tights. Wear cotton knickers and cotton or wool tights to allow skin here to breathe more easily.

Illusions

Remember that women, unlike little girls and boys or men, are meant to have fattier areas around their rear ends. It's what makes them curvy and woman-like! If you feel that your bottom is just too big, see the posture and clothes section in Chapter 3 to help give you a firmer, slimmer look. Choose knickers that fit around your bottom so that they don't create a line over it under clothes and draw attention to it. Opt for a straight top, like a long T-shirt or jumper which reaches just below your bottom, with a tight fitting skirt or leggings, to disguise a large behind. Avoid very tight-fitting trousers, leggings or jeans around your backside - they'll make it look bigger. And always check your back view when buying fitted clothes and trousers.

TROUBLE-SHOOTING

Q: *I'm so ashamed. I can't stop biting my nails. They look horrible and I feel silly doing it. How can I stop?*

A: Have you tried things that taste disgusting on them? There are special ones available for nail biting at the chemist which are not noticeable. Or put some scent of foods you don't like on them – the juice of canned carrots, a little rhubarb juice etc; whatever you really hate. Have you tried wearing gloves a lot in cold weather (to protect those poor, abused nails)? Have you tried chewing gum instead? And have you tried making your nails look as best as they can with regular manicures and nail polish, so you won't feel like making them look so horrible?

If all this has failed and you can't even start to be proud of them, you may like to take a tip from one of the most photographed women in the world who used to bite her nails. You'll need a little help from your mum for this. Ask her if, as a birthday or Christmas present, you can go and have false nails bonded on. Unlike the awful talons of the past, false nails can now be made to look natural and short so no one except you and the manicurist will know the difference. They are bonded on to your nails so they shouldn't come off for weeks, and they will give yours a chance to grow underneath. They're also, apparently, not very satisfying to chew. Then you can start being proud of your hands, giving yourself regular manicures and hopefully the habit will be broken. Fingers crossed!

Q: *People often talk about going to beauticians, but what can they do for me that I can't do at home?*

A: Well, first and foremost it's a complete luxury to be pampered, and especially in surroundings where no one will interrupt you or you suddenly feel you must do those practical things you'd forgotten about until now. So apart from the body benefiting, going to a beautician can make you feel calmer and more relaxed, especially if you go for something like a facial massage or body aromatherapy; these are the most popular beauty treatments of all. You can massage yourself in a quiet moment at home, of course, but it's not quite as relaxing when you have to find out how to do it effectively and then think about what you're doing. These people are experts and your mind can wander while you feel the benefits.

Beauticians are also trained to assess your skin and help combat any problems it has. Some people can do this themselves but it's not easy to see yourself objectively or clearly from all angles close up. A good beautician can give you deeper treatments with potions that they have devoted time and energy to finding out how to use. On a more practical side, they can use equipment like massage machines and electrolysis that are extremely expensive and just wouldn't be worth one person buying. So people go to beauty salons to relax and get expert advice and treatment. A gift voucher for a beauty treatment is a wonderful present to give or receive.

Q: ***I look like Santa Claus. I've got the chubbiest cheeks I've ever seen. Is there any way to make them look slimmer and show my cheekbones?***

A: There are some tricks. But first let me tell you that you have the kind of face that won't wrinkle or look older so fast when you get there. Wide and rounder faces keep on looking younger for longer. You'll be pleased at the time. Honestly!

Now for some illusions. Look at the make-up section to find out how to magic in some cheekbones with darker shading. Also make sure that eye make-up, like pencil and shadow if you use it, goes slightly up at the outside of your lids (towards your brows) to look as if there's some cheekbone at the side. Do the same with your hair. Keep it wide at cheekbone and temple level, either by a cut that has a definite strong layer there or by styling longer hair with some bounce out at that place. If you wear earrings make them large and close to the ear so that it takes attention horizontally across your face instead of round the outline as dangly ones would. Wear lower or 'V' shapes around your neckline to suggest angles and a longer neck which will make your face look less round. Happy trickery!

Q: ***Please help me. I've been told I've got to wear glasses and they look totally stupid on me. Boys hate them, I know.***

A: Who told you boys hate glasses? Do you know any boys who wear glasses? Do they look stupid? Or does it give them an attractive intellectual air? It can do the same for you. Take a look around at girls who wear glasses – the ones that you don't like are probably the ones which haven't been chosen well. There are lots of options with prescription lenses, so you can have them tinted in different shades or they can be light sensitive to darken in the sun to look more like sunglasses outside. And many prescription glasses are now 'off the peg' in big chemists so you can save up and collect a wardrobe of them for different occasions and outfits. Also some chemists and opticians do a two-for-one deal, so you buy one and get a second pair free. Shop around and perhaps make that second pair a bit more stylish or fun (small wire frames, shocking pink plastic ones, mock tortoiseshell). For the everyday pair, you need to choose your frames carefully to fit your colouring and face shape. Here are the guidelines:
Colour and size: If you have fair features, a small face and/or a neat, fine or swept-back hairstyle, go for lighter and finer frames so they don't look bolder than the rest of your face. Bigger faces, darker colouring and bold or big hairstyles can take brighter, deeper and larger frames.
Shape: The tops should follow the line

of your eyebrows and they should not stick out further than your temples at the sides. A high bridge across the glasses will make your nose look longer. Lower wider bridges are better for large or bigger noses. Round faces need squarer frames to balance and not emphasise the roundness. Squarer jawlines look better with rounded or sideways pear-shaped frames. If you have a large forehead and pointed chin (heart-shaped face) opt for lighter, small shapes so as not to bring attention to the top area of your face. A long face looks better with heavier, wider and rounded frames to give the appearance of widening them. Oval frames suit most face shapes.

After that it's trial and error. When you try frames on, get an overall impression by looking at them from the side and three quarter view, too. And make sure that they feel comfortable. Find some stylish changeable spectacle ropes, which double up as necklaces, to hold your glasses when you take them off.

By the way, have you considered contact lenses? There are all sorts of different types now, which are easier to wear once you get used to putting them in. If you want to have fun there are even coloured ones in prescription lenses so you can change your eye colour (or brighten it up) at the same time (see above). Have fun with your new accessory!

Q: ***I hate my hands and feet. They're huge! Whenever I'm with people I try to hide them away which can be awkward. Help me make them smaller.***

A: I'm sorry but no one can make them smaller. They are part of how you are; but you can make the best of them (see our hands and feet section in this chapter). It sounds to me as though you're not very confident with yourself anyway, despite the hands and feet. We all have bits of ourselves we'd like to hide, and we're all different, but as I've said earlier, that's what makes us fascinating as individuals. I'm pretty sure that no one who meets you says, 'Wow, look at her enormous hands or feet!'. They're much more likely to be thinking 'I wonder why she looks so sad or unfriendly'. By trying to hide away bits of yourself you're withdrawing from people, so try this instead: next time you go out forget about your hands and feet. Instead wear something particularly to highlight and show up a bit of you that you're proud of – a bold skinny dress for your great figure, a sparkly pair of earrings to show off your nice eyes (or neck if they're dangly), or a fine metallic headband through your fabulous hair. Wear it with a big smile to show how friendly you'd like to be. Shake hands or put your arm round someone – dance – they're much more likely to notice your warmth and vitality than what you're doing it with!

Also remember that everyone feels under confident sometimes – so admire things you like about others and help boost their confidence, too.

The End